YORK NOTES

Thomas Hardy

THE RETURN OF THE NATIVE

Notes by Stewart Luke

BA (ADELAIDE) *Senior Lecturer in English Adelaide College of the Arts and Education*

LONGMAN
YORK PRESS

YORK PRESS
Immeuble Esseily, Place Riad Solh, Beirut.

LONGMAN GROUP LIMITED
London
Associated companies, branches and representatives throughout the world

First published 1980
ISBN 0 582 78112 4
Printed in Hong Kong by
Wilture Enterprises (International) Ltd

Contents

Part 1

Introduction

THOMAS HARDY was born in Dorset in 1840. Nearly all his novels are set in Dorset in the south of England. The whole of the south-western area of England he called Wessex, which is an old name for it. Dorset is a part of Wessex. The Wessex he describes in his later novels is 'a modern Wessex of railways, the penny post, mowing and reaping machines, union work-houses, lucifer matches, labourers who could read and write, and National school children'.* The Wessex he describes in *The Return of the Native* is the heath country which is quite useless for growing anything because the soil is a light sand.

Farming is not possible on Egdon. People live by cutting turf or furze, or making brooms. Rural Wessex is slow and old fashioned. It is as though time has stopped. Diggory Venn makes a living by selling reddle which is a red earthy substance used by farmers for marking sheep. It is not a dead area, however, because there are heath-croppers, butterflies, ants, rabbits and snakes.

As a boy his long walks to school brought him close to the country and its customs. One of his family's favourite walks was to Rainbarrow where Hardy's father would look through a telescope at the surrounding country. Hardy himself loved to look at things from a distance or a height as he does in *The Return of the Native*. His father introduced him to the business world of the stone mason and to nature; his mother introduced him to history and legend. Family and local history interested him much more than what went on in the world at large. His parents sometimes told him stories of violence which haunted him because he had a sensitive, morbid nature. On one occasion he watched with interest the public hanging of a woman. His curiosity was abnormal. He loved animals and small creatures which seemed to him to have a timelessness that man did not. A good example in *The Return of the Native* is Mrs Yeobright's description of the ants.

Hardy hated physical contact. He did not like to be touched. As a boy he was precocious, he liked older company, and loved playing the fiddle. He was quietly spoken, well read, and ambitious. Of himself Hardy said 'that a clue to much of his character and action throughout his life is afforded by his lateness of development in virility'.† He was always reticent about his sexual life. Who is to blame him?

*Preface to *Far from the Madding Crowd*, 1895.

†F. E. Hardy, *Life of Thomas Hardy*, Volume 1, Macmillan, London, 1962, p.32.

At sixteen he was apprenticed to an architect and spent all his spare time in study. When he moved to London the young country boy was shocked by office conversations and by open prostitution in Cremorne Gardens. London was the right place for him to enjoy the music he loved so much and to acquire more knowledge. He appears to have been a keen collector of information. Hardy grew bored by his architectural training because it was too mechanical and because, being a young man from the country, he did not have the social contacts necessary to enable him to gain contracts from the wealthy. After a year in London he decided to return to literature and his own education. Architecture became a secondary interest. His first love was poetry, and he was determined to master the craft of fiction.

In 1867 he returned to Dorset for health reasons as an architect's assistant. Here he wrote the draft of his first novel *The Poor Man and the Lady*. Macmillan, the publisher, rejected it and Hardy later destroyed it. He remained determined to succeed as a writer. *Desperate Remedies* (1871) was his first novel to be published. It was an edition of five hundred copies and Hardy had to pay seventy-five pounds towards the cost. Reviews were mixed but at least he was praised for his ability to describe nature and create authentic local atmosphere. Hardy, who was continuing his work restoring churches, was desperately short of money. Then he was invited to publish *A Pair of Blue Eyes* (1873) in serial form in monthly parts in *Tinsley's Magazine*. He was glad to accept. It proved to be good practice for him in overcoming the difficulties and mastering the art of serial writing.

Leslie Stephen, the editor of the *Cornhill Magazine*, volunteered in 1872 to publish his next novel which was to be *Far from the Madding Crowd*. His friend and tutor Horace Moule killed himself while Hardy was at work on the novel. This is the last of Hardy's novels with a happy ending. From now on his heroes and heroines become tragic figures. In 1874 he married Emma Gifford. His intellect attracted her; her vitality attracted him. Their first home was at Sturminster where he wrote *The Return of the Native*, which was by far his best novel to date. Today it remains one of his most popular despite its intense gloom.

Later novels well worth reading are *The Mayor of Casterbridge* (1886), *The Woodlanders* (1887), and especially *Tess of the d'Urbervilles* (1891) and *Jude the Obscure* (1896). Because the last one caused such a public outcry Hardy decided to write no more novels. He devoted the rest of his life to writing poetry. Although his marriage with Emma Gifford had not been particularly happy, when she died he wrote one of the finest series of love poems in the English language.

The year the First World War broke out he married again and worked on his collections of verse until he died in 1928. His ashes were buried in Westminster Abbey.

Hardy wrote regional novels—narratives confined to a district. Great Britain is a small island. Its inhabitants are insular in outlook. It is natural for writers to choose local settings because they know them and because they think they are important. The regional or country novel was common in England in the nineteenth century, and the outlook of the English novelist is narrow compared with that of, say, the Russian who takes a broad view. Some people still thought that God made the country and man made the town.

Hardy did not think that to confine his novels to Wessex was to limit them in any way. What happens in Wessex is what happens elsewhere. The tensions, conflicts, and dilemmas that people experience here are common to mankind. And he believed that what happened to people in a local district could be presented in such a way as to have universal application and appeal.

There was a tradition of country writing behind him. For example there is Jane Austen's *Emma* (1816), in which polite people talk to one another and arrange marriages in country houses; there is Elizabeth Gaskell's *Cranford* (1853), in which old ladies take tea according to the rules of etiquette; there are Trollope's novels about church affairs in Barsetshire; there is George Eliot's *Silas Marner* (1861), about town and country. Perhaps the best known regional novelist after Hardy is D.H. Lawrence, who in *The Rainbow* (1915) and *Women in Love* (1921) explores male-female relationships and society in the Nottinghamshire-Derbyshire border area.

Of course, Hardy does not choose to describe the country of Wessex just for the sake of description. He does it so that we can see men and women living in a landscape that is timeless and unchangeable. Wessex is a district full of history, legend, and folklore. It has its own local customs such as bonfires and Maypole festivities, its own superstitions about witches and reddlemen, and its own quaint habits of speech. Wessex is a character itself.

Because Hardy's world occupies such a small area, the characters live near one another and frequently meet one another. That accounts for some of the complaints about coincidence in Hardy's novels. It is inevitable that his characters bump into one another. They don't meet by chance. They just cannot help meeting. Hardy said that by limiting the action of the novel to Egdon Heath he created a 'unity of place . . . seldom preserved in novels', and he provided his readers with a map of the area. He also wanted a unity of time because the action was to take a year and a day. At the back of his mind were the Greek tragedies of Aeschylus and Sophocles. *The Return of the Native* is the first novel in which he incorporates such features of tragedy. It was obviously very difficult for him to impose a tragic structure on a novel published in serial form. And tragedy was Hardy's natural inclination. In the preface to *The Return of the Native* he is pleased to think that Egdon might be 'the heath of that traditionary King of Wessex—Lear'.

References to tragic figures such as Oedipus are frequent in the novel. Clym Yeobright, however, has neither the stature nor depth of character to be a tragic figure. He is often silly and he is often a bore. Eustacia Vye comes closer to being a tragic figure who engages our sympathy. But at times instead of being a heroine or goddess or *femme fatale* she is simply a silly young girl with silly ideas.

In writing the novel Hardy was not setting out to prove anything. He believed that a novel should not argue a case for or against something. Instead it should be an impression—a writer's impression of life. Hardy's impression in *The Return of the Native* is that family relationships are tragic, that people who try to rise above their class are doomed, that country characters will survive doing what they have been doing for centuries, and that nothing will change.

Hardy believed that no story was worth writing unless it were exceptional or unusual. A reader is not interested in the dreary description of everyday commonplace events, however real or true they may be. He believed that the novelist should satisfy the reader's 'love of the uncommon in human experience'. There is an abundance of uncommon events in *The Return of the Native.* He also thought that the writer had to strike a balance between the portrayal of ordinary life and the portrayal of a life that is extraordinary. If the novelist did not do this his story would be unreal, unconvincing, too strange. The characters themselves must be convincing. They cannot be abnormal because the reader has to recognise them as part of human nature; as people in whom he believes. The unusual in fiction, then, must be in the events and not the characters. The meeting of lovers under an eclipse of the moon, games of dice at night on a heath, an old woman's walk to death on a heath, and the burning of an effigy are not common events.

The novel became the most widely read literary form in the nineteenth century because it was the best means of portraying the life of the middle classes who had acquired money and power and who had leisure to read. Lending libraries flourished and magazines which included serials were popular. The novelist knew his reader and knew what he wanted to read because he shared his views on religion, love, status, ambition, marital status, and fortune. He also had a similar background to his reader.

The social history of England in the nineteenth century is in the novels. Take a sample published in one decade and you will find that they highlight the values of English society. (Such a sample might include Dickens, *The Mystery of Edwin Drood* (1870); George Eliot, *Middlemarch* (1871–1872); Meredith, *The Egoist* (1879); Trollope, *The Way We Live Now* (1875); and Hardy, *The Return of the Native* (1878)).

During this period the more powerful and newly rich middle classes were competing with the old aristocracy for power. In English fiction you will often find the old nobility presented as eccentrics, sources of amusement, pompous asses, gluttons, lecherous old men and flirtatious old women. Invariably they are comic figures because the novelists are Whigs whose point of view we are invited to adopt. It is also true of course that the old aristocracy was stupid and gross and sat on its inherited land in complacent unawareness of the poverty around it and of the hardships it imposed.

Hardy is more interested in human aspirations and relationships than he is in social criticism. Love, marriage, and the family are central to his novels. He was also the first English novelist to explore male-female relationships outside marriage. This caused scandal in a Victorian society which pretended in public that sex did not exist and which acted in private as it saw fit. *Tess of the d'Urbervilles* and *Jude the Obscure* in particular aroused public indignation. Alterations were even made to *The Return of the Native* to obscure the relationship between Eustacia Vye and Damon Wildeve before the novel starts.

A note on the text

The Return of the Native first appeared in serial form in twelve parts in the *Belgravia* magazine in 1878. Later that year the novel was published in book form. Hardy made some alterations to this first edition when it appeared in 1895 as volume six of the Uniform Edition of his novels. He tries to make Clym Yeobright more modern by giving him a knowledge of French and German rather than the classics; he makes Eustacia more romantic by giving her a Corfiote background; he compares her with Sappho and not Marie Antoinette as in the first edition. Here too Eustacia had said to Damon of their love affair 'as if I had never been yours'. In the 1895 edition she says 'as if I had never been yours body and soul so irretrievably'. When the novel appeared as volume four of the Wessex Edition, Macmillan, London, 1912, Hardy had changed the phrase 'body and soul' to 'life and soul'.

The Wessex is the best edition of *The Return of the Native*. Macmillan, London, first published the New Wessex Edition in paperback in 1974, with an introduction and notes by Derwent May.

Part 2

Summaries

of THE RETURN OF THE NATIVE

A general summary

Egdon Heath is timeless, cold, impersonal and ominous. 'Every night its Titanic form seemed to await something'. Something is going to happen and the tone of the opening chapter suggests that it will be tragic. Egdon is timeless; people are not.

Egdon looks on as the reddleman, his cart, and Captain Vye make their way along the dry, white road. The characters are dwarfed in the landscape. They are but specks. In the cart is Thomasin who has run away from Wildeve and is returning to the house of her aunt Mrs Yeobright. The marriage ceremony could not be performed because of an irregularity in the licence. It was rather foolish of Wildeve, former engineer and now keeper of The Quiet Woman, not to have noticed that the licence was made out for Budmouth and not Anglebury.

Nearby on a barrow, an ancient burial mound, which 'formed the pole and axis of this heathery world', stood a female figure who seemed to dominate the landscape as the queen of solitude. It is 5 November, and the local people, or rustics, who earn a living by cutting furze and entertain themselves by dancing, are commemorating the Gunpowder Plot by lighting fires. In their conversations the rustics introduce us to the main characters in the novel—Eustacia Vye, Clym Yeobright, Thomasin Yeobright and Wildeve.

Clym, born on Egdon, went to Paris where he was successful as manager to a diamond merchant, and is now about to return to his native soil; hence the title of the novel. Eustacia Vye has been having a secret love-affair with Damon Wildeve only because there was nobody better around. Her fire and her witch-like power summon him to Rainbarrow that same November night, where Johnny Nunsuch overhears their conversation and later reports it to the reddleman. Diggory Venn once proposed to Thomasin, was rejected, abandoned his dairy farm, and became a reddleman. He acts as her guardian angel throughout the novel.

On the way to Eustacia's house the reddleman sees a wild mallard (a duck) which looks as though it is thinking 'that a present moment of comfortable reality is worth a decade of memories'. The bird has knowledge, is miserable, and suffers. Hardy develops the theme that people who have knowledge and think must suffer. There is little comfort for the characters in this novel. Venn flatters Eustacia, asks her to give up Wildeve so that he will marry Thomasin more quickly, and offers her a job in Budmouth, a place in her dreams—'a great salt sheening sea bending into the land like a bow—thousands of gentle-people walking up and down—bands of music playing—officers by sea and officers by land walking among the rest'. Eustacia, however much she loved the idea of Budmouth, would not be told or advised what to do. She wants Wildeve more now because somebody else has claim to him. Wildeve wants her now when he learns that another man loves Thomasin. Eustacia then sees Wildeve through different eyes. 'And you come to get me because you cannot get her. This is certainly a new position altogether. I am happy to be a stop-gap.' As soon as she thinks that the other woman does not want Wildeve she doesn't want him either. There is no glamour or glory in a reject. It is certainly not Eustacia's style to accept cast-offs or hand-me-downs. There is a touch of the perverse in her 'supersubtle, epicurean heart'. Wildeve has become superfluous. The first book, 'The Three Women', ends with Captain Vye's announcement that Clym Yeobright is coming home for Christmas from the pomp and vanity of Paris.

Eustacia overhears two of the rustics conversing with Captain Vye as they build a stack of furze-faggots. They say that Clym is educated and for that reason has strange notions. Moreover if children were not taught how to write they would not go around writing dirty words on doors and gateposts. They also think that Eustacia and Clym would make a fine pair. Eustacia's imagination goes to work making her inner world 'as animated as water under a microscope'. The nineteen-year-old dreamer goes to look at Clym's house at Blooms-End that night.

Clym bids her good evening in the dark and she goes home to dream of a knight in shining armour. Already Eustacia has conjured up a vision with which to fall in love. Her passion is of the imagination. She needs a grand passion.

'"Ah," she said to herself, "want of an object to live for—that's all is the matter with me"'. Wildeve has become inadequate. She needs a hero of her own creation. In order to get into the Yeobright party she takes Charley's part in the play of *St George* and allows Charley to hold her hand for a while. When she meets Clym she is troubled by his appearance and is drawn to him because she had talked herself into it in advance. They have a silly, stilted conversation and she forgets an appointment with Wildeve. Eustacia returns gifts and sends a letter by the reddleman to Wildeve who charges off to arrange a marriage with Thomasin. Diggory Venn loses again.

Although Thomasin realises that Wildeve is not perfect she still wants to marry him. And after all, her pride has been hurt, and Clym, in his tedious conventional way, thinks that she has been jilted on her wedding day. She would like to allay his fear and leaves the house to marry Wildeve half an hour before Clym returns from visiting friends. Eustacia gives her away and while Thomasin was signing her name 'Wildeve had flung towards Eustacia a glance that said plainly, "I have punished you now"'. Her reply was heartfelt. 'You mistake; it gives me sincerest pleasure to see her your wife today.' The reddleman leaves Egdon Heath for many months. There is no more that he can do.

Eustacia, hoping to see Clym, goes to church. Susan Nunsuch pricks her arm with a long stocking-needle to draw blood and put an end to what she thinks is the bewitching of her children. Clym has decided to abandon Paris and set up a school on Egdon for the improvement of the locals. His mother and the locals think he is foolish. We know he is because Hardy insists on it. After hearing of Eustacia's misfortune in church, and after Sam the furze-cutter has fired his imagination with an account of the handsome girl, Clym wonders if she would be interested in schoolteaching. Sam, like all the other rustics, who are practical people, knows better. He says that her thoughts are far away from Egdon 'with lords and ladies she'll never know, and mansions she'll never see again'. The voice of truth often comes from the ordinary people in this novel.

After Clym has helped the rustics to remove a bucket from Captain Vye's well, Hardy introduces a few ominous touches. Clym sees the ashes of the November bonfire. Eustacia throws a stone in the pool. There is a splash. Wildeve does not appear. Then there is an unlikely but important conversation between Eustacia and Clym in which she says that she does not have much love for her fellow-creatures, does not want to teach, she hates nature, that for her the heath can be endured only when the heather is out, and that the streets of Paris attract her. Clym, who has finished with Paris, would rather live on Egdon than anywhere else in the world because it is 'exhilarating, and strengthening, and soothing'. The seeds of conflict have been sown. Mrs Yeobright tries to discourage him from seeing Eustacia but he presses on to the excavated barrow to find a present of human bones for his beloved.

Under an eclipse of the moon they embrace on Rainbarrow. It is a striking romantic movement in the novel. Unfortunately the magic is dispelled by the absurdity of their melodramatic conversation. She goes home and Clym considers his dilemma: he wants to restore his mother's trust in him, he wants to make Eustacia happy, and he wants to teach. 'My plan is one for instilling high knowledge into empty minds without first cramming them with what has to be uncrammed again before true study begins.' Mrs Yeobright thinks he is silly and that he is destroying himself. They argue about Eustacia. Clym decides to leave home and marry her. On the way to his cottage he notices the harsh punishment inflicted on the beech trees by the June rains. Even the finch cannot sing. Clym does seem to be going the wrong way. His mother harps on his 'steady opposition and persistence in going wrong'. Thomasin further distresses her with the knowledge that Wildeve refuses to give her money to buy things she needs. When Wildeve learns of the forthcoming marriage he wants Eustacia again.

He goes to Mrs Yeobright's to collect a gift for Thomasin. She does not trust him to take the guineas she has promised Thomasin and instead sends Christian Cantle with them so that Thomasin and Clym may share the present on his wedding day. Christian meets Fairway and others who persuade him to go to The Quiet Woman to take part in a raffle. He wins a gown-piece. Wildeve discovers he is carrying money for his wife and accompanies him out of the inn in a state of anger. The reddleman, who happens to be in the inn, follows them on to the heath where Christian loses all the money to Wildeve by playing dice. In one of the most unusual scenes in the book, the reddleman wins the money from Wildeve, and gives it to Thomasin not realising that half of it belongs to Clym.

Mrs Yeobright, led to believe that Wildeve had given Clym's share to Eustacia, challenges her. They have a bitter quarrel. Eustacia never wants to see her again. Clym thinks they will never be friends. 'Well, what must be will be.' Eustacia asks Clym to take her away from Egdon to Paris but he decides to work even harder at his books. His night studies cause acute inflammation of the eyes. He becomes an invalid in a darkened room for three weeks. Reading is out of the question and he decides to be a furze- and turf-cutter. The man of promise who went to Paris has returned to his native soil with a vengeance in adopting the humblest occupation on Egdon. Eustacia is shocked to find him content in his new work. She feels humiliated because he does not regard himself as a social failure. Her pride is badly hurt. In her eyes he should be cursing, not singing at his work. Clym is satisfied because it gives him something to do and enables him to earn a little money. His explanation does not satisfy Eustacia:

> 'Now, don't you suppose, my inexperienced girl, that I cannot rebel, in high Promethean fashion, against the gods and fate as well as you. I have felt more steam and smoke of that sort than you have ever heard of. But the more I see of life the more I perceive that there is nothing particularly great in its greatest walks, and therefore nothing particularly small in mine of furze-cutting.'

Married for two months, they are already estranged. Her hero from Paris is now only a poor man in brown leather who cannot see properly.

Eustacia shows how wayward and capricious she is by going to the local festivities and dancing with Wildeve. She drifts off on a cloud of fantasy as she enjoys the dance, the moonlight, the secrecy, and perhaps Wildeve, who enjoys the forbidden fruit at his side. He says that Fate has been unkind to her and walks part of the way home with her. The reddleman sees them together. Later on the heath, he fires a gun near Wildeve to frighten him off Eustacia. What the return of the native means to Eustacia is now quite clear:

> 'If you had never returned to your native place, Clym, what a blessing it would have been for you! . . . It has altered the destinies of—'
>
> 'Three people.'
>
> 'Five', Eustacia thought; but she kept that in.

To attempt a reconciliation with her son and his wife Mrs Yeobright walks across the heath in the August heat. She follows the figure of a furze-cutter who happens to be Clym. It is a melancholy scene. The narrative is restrained. There is no external comment or intrusion from Hardy. The effect is haunting and poignant. Exhausted, she sits down under some trees, and observes a man enter Clym's cottage.

Wildeve in his new summer suit talks to Eustacia while Clym the furze-cutter lies asleep on the floor. She feels bitter, cheated. The dream of the happy life she hoped to share with Clym has evaporated. She is despairing and frustrated. 'But do I desire unreasonably much in wanting what is called life—music, poetry, passion, war, and all the beating and pulsing that is going on in the greatest arteries of the world?'. Her dreams and fancies have vanished. Mrs Yeobright knocks at the door. Eustacia decides not to open it because she thinks Mrs Yeobright has come to see Clym and not her, whom she dislikes. She knocks again. Eustacia hears Clym stirring and saying 'Mother', assumes that he will open the door, and goes out of the back door with Wildeve. On returning to the house she finds Clym still asleep, and on opening the door she does not find Mrs Yeobright.

With her eyes fixed on the ground Mrs Yeobright hastens across the heath brooding over Clym's hook and brambles lying at the door and Eustacia's face at the window. She has been turned away. She thinks aloud in the company of Johnny Nunsuch, who gets her some water and who is told to tell his mother that he has seen 'a broken-hearted woman cast off by her son'. Clym wakes after dreaming that he went to his mother's house but couldn't get in even though she was crying for help. In the evening he heads for his mother's house and finds her lying on the heath. They reach a disused hut where Clym and the rustics discover she has been bitten by an adder. Eustacia, on her way to meet Clym, blames Fate for her unhappy lot, learns of Wildeve's place in the sun in the form of an inheritance, meets Wildeve and comes upon the hut. Mrs Yeobright dies of exhaustion and snake bite and Johnny Nunsuch relates her last words.

Clym is distraught and becomes ill. He is out of his senses for a week, four days of calm follow, then there is remorse, guilt, despair. Thomasin thinks the time is not right to tell him that his mother came to his door. Clym learns of his mother's journey from Christian, of her intention to forgive from the reddleman, and of her visit to his house from Johnny Nunsuch. 'Beware the fury of a patient man' rings in our ears. During this human anguish the heath remains imperturbable, impassive. Clym confronts Eustacia who tells him what happened but will not reveal the name of the man with her. The scene is torture for both of them. They separate. Eustacia returns to her grandfather's where Charley looks after her in distress. He hides the pistols she has been looking at too long.

It is 5 November again. Charley lights a bonfire to divert and entertain her. Wildeve interprets it as the old signal, a stone splashes in the pond, he arrives and offers help. She suggests that he might help her escape to Budmouth to get a boat across the Channel to France and then Paris. She does not know whether she wants him as a friend or as a lover and will signal him some night at eight o'clock. Clym sits in his mother's house wishing Eustacia would come; she wishes he would come. She makes preparations for flight; he writes a letter welcoming her back. There is a frenzied hopelessness about her preparations. 'She had used to think of the heath alone as an uncongenial spot to be in; she felt it now of the whole world.' She sends a signal to which Wildeve replies. He will drive her to Budmouth at midnight. Clym's letter is left in the parlour but she misses it on her way out to the appointment.

As Eustacia staggers through the chaos of the night on the heath Susan Nunsuch makes a wax image of her. As the image melts Eustacia walks on. Thomasin arrives with her baby to warn Clym that Wildeve is about to run away with Eustacia. Clym and Captain Vye head for The Quiet Woman. Thomasin follows with her baby and comes upon the reddleman who has heard Eustacia crying near his van. A splash is heard in the weir, Clym and Wildeve rush to Eustacia's rescue, then the reddleman rushes to their rescue. After the climax of the novel Diggory Venn sits by the fire in the inn reflecting on the course of events on Egdon. Eustacia and Wildeve are dead. Clym just escaped:

> The last occasion on which he had lingered by that fireplace was when the raffle was in progress; when Wildeve was alive and well; Thomasin active and smiling in the next room; Yeobright and Eustacia just made husband and wife, and Mrs Yeobright living at Blooms-End . . . of all the circle, he himself was the only one whose situation had not materially changed.

His mood is calm, nostalgic, sad. Clym is in torment because he feels responsible for the deaths of two women and no law can punish him.

In the final section 'Aftercourses', Thomasin marries the reddleman and Clym delivers Sermons on the Mount on the barrow where Eustacia had stood. At nearly thirty-three Clym has found his new vocation as a preacher.

Detailed summaries

BOOK FIRST: THE THREE WOMEN

Chapter 1: A Face on which Time makes but little impression

The setting of the novel is Egdon Heath which is dark, sinister, and brooding. Hardy uses long words and clumsy phrases to describe it. The prose style is awkward and stilted. He is trying to develop ideas which will become themes in the novel:

(1) Egdon Heath is permanent.
(2) Egdon Heath has a savage intensity.
(3) Its solemn beauty is more in keeping with the modern age.
(4) Like modern man it has 'a lonely face, suggesting tragical possibilities'.

For a discussion of Egdon see pages 59–62.

NOTES AND GLOSSARY:

furze-cutter: somebody who gathers the branches of a shrub called furze for fuel

faggot: a bundle of twigs

opacity: darkness

Titanic: in Greek mythology the Titans were the children of Uranus, the sky, and Ge, the earth. Hardy means that the heath is vast and that it has the qualities of the dark underworld of Tartarus into which the Titans were thrown

the final overthrow: an ambiguous phrase with a sinister note. Does it mean the end of the world?

Vale of Tempe: a beautiful valley in Greece

Thule: the bleakest area in the north of the world. Hardy means that people today will find more beauty in Thule than in any Vale of Tempe because ideas of beauty have changed and because people feel closer to the stark and the bleak

Heidelberg and Baden: pleasant tourist resorts in Germany

Scheveningen: a wind-swept tourist resort on the Dutch coast

ascetic: somebody who practises strict self-discipline

summer days of highest feather: the best of summer days
Domesday: the Domesday Book was the official survey of the lands of England ordered by William the Conqueror in 1086
Leland: employed by Henry VIII, John Leland reported on the state of the country in 1534
Ishmaelitish: in the Bible, Ishmael, eldest son of Abraham, was banished to the wilderness (Genesis 16:12). Hardy means that Egdon is an area for outcasts and is an outcast itself
an anomalous look: that is, looks out of place
barrow: an ancient heap of earth or stones over a grave
vicinal way: not a main but a local road
Via Iceniana, or Ikenild Street: Icknield Way, a main road built by the Romans in England

Chapter 2: Humanity appears upon the Scene, Hand in Hand with Trouble

An old man meets a reddleman driving his cart along the white road across the heath. Hardy creates a feeling of mystery and suspense that makes the reader want to read on. Who is the old man? What is the young girl doing in the cart? What kind of person is the strange reddleman? Through his eyes we look at the barrow and detect a solitary female figure. 'The imagination of the observer clung by preference to that vanished, solitary figure, as to something more interesting, more important, more likely to have a history worth knowing than these newcomers.' Who is she?

NOTES AND GLOSSARY:
reddleman: the redding he sells to farmers for marking their sheep is a red ochre
acclivities: steep slopes
Atlantean: in Greek mythology Atlas was one of the earth-giants. Hardy again emphasises the vastness of the heath
Celts: ancient inhabitants of Britain
tumulus: barrow (see note on Chapter 1, above)

Chapter 3: The Custom of the Country

In this very long chapter Hardy introduces us to the rustics who are lighting a bonfire on 5 November. They develop the plot further by introducing the reader to Clym Yeobright, Captain Vye and his daughter, and Mrs Yeobright, and by giving the reader the history of the relationship between Damon Wildeve and Thomasin Yeobright. It is their intention to celebrate the marriage they think has taken place that day. They talk in a Wessex dialect which can be hard to follow.

NOTES AND GLOSSARY:

hamlets: villages

Maenades: in Greek mythology, the wild priestesses of Bacchus, the God of wine. Some of the fires have a drunken wildness about them

ephemeral: short lived

Limbo: Dante Alighieri (1265–1321), Italy's major poet, describes Limbo in his *Divine Comedy* as being a place near hell inhabited by people who died before the time of Christ and by unbaptised children

the sublime Florentine: Dante was born in Florence

'souls of mighty worth': Hardy is quoting from Dante: 'well I knew/ Suspended in that Limbo many a soul/ Of mighty worth' (Canto 4)

Thor and Woden: Scandinavian gods of war, wisdom, and of the dead

Druidical: Druids were learned priests in ancient Britain and Gaul

Saxon: an ancient tribe, originally German, of which one portion, the Anglo Saxons, settled in Britain in the fifth and sixth centuries

Gunpowder Plot: there was a plot to blow up the British Houses of Parliament with gunpowder in which Guy Fawkes was involved. It failed. Each year on 5 November, children in Britain used to celebrate Guy Fawkes' Day by lighting bonfires and fireworks. Because fireworks are considered more dangerous than they used to be, the custom is less common now. Hardy means that the rustics are lighting a bonfire not for Guy Fawkes in particular. They light it as part of a tradition handed down to them from ancient times. And they light it as an act of defiance in the face of approaching winter

Promethean: Prometheus, in Greek mythology, was the son of an earth-giant or Titan, and stole fire from heaven and brought it to earth against the wishes of Zeus

fiat: instruction. Latin *fiat lux* = let there be light (Genesis 1:3)

Durereseque: refers to Albrecht Dürer (1471–1528), the German painter

'The king . . . may be': a seventeenth-century ballad

'I'll go shrive the queen': 'I'll go and hear the queen's confession'
wend: go
a boon: something to be thankful for
stave: song
weasand: throat
'Dostn't wish th' wast three sixes again, Grandfer?': 'don't you wish you were eighteen again, Grandfather?'
'There's a hole in thy poor bellows': 'your lungs aren't so strong as they used to be'
jowned: blessed or damned
'neither yell nor mark have been seen of 'em since': there has been no sign of them since!
vell: skin
forbad the banns: public notice used to be given in a church of an intended marriage. Anyone who objected to the union said so in church. As Thomasin's guardian, Mrs Yeobright stops the union because she does not think Damon Wildeve is a suitable partner
set-to: arrangement or relationship
mangling: developing or going on
Philistine: in the Bible, 1 Samuel 17:6, the giant Philistine slain by David wore brass armour on his legs
nunny-watch: fuss
banging: impressive
to-year: this year
here-right: right here in our district
tide-times: times of religious celebrations such as Christmas time
close: secret
victuals: food and drink
chiel: child
'couldn't use to make a round O to save their bones from the pit': couldn't write a single letter even if their lives depended on it
Bang-up Locals: the impressive Dorset Yeomanry
the year four: 1804
zid: saw
mark: somebody who can't write and puts a cross for his name
dog-days: the hottest time of the year
strawmote: a single blade of corn
stunpoll: fool
gallicrow: scarecrow
maphrotight: hermaphrodite, somebody with the characteristics of both sexes

tatie-digging: the time of year when potatoes are harvested
book of judgment: the church record of baptisms
Lammas-tide: 1 August was a harvest festival in the early English Church
rames: skeleton
wethers: castrated male sheep
ballet: ballad
kex: dry, hollow stem of a plant
nammet-time: lunch eaten in the fields
cleft-wood: wood that has been chopped
knap: hill
zany: fool
dandy: attractive
hare eyes: popping eyes
outstep: remote, out of the way
numskull: silly head
mandy: cheeky
vlankers: sparks of fire
vagary: a spontaneous prank
poussetted: danced round with hands joined
mommet: an effigy or strange figure
Nebo: the mountain from which Moses looked at the promised land. Mrs Yeobright has a superior air suggesting that she knows more than others
huffle: blow in sudden gusts
pixy-led: led astray by fairies

Chapter 4: The Halt on the Turnpike Road

Mrs Yeobright is perplexed and angry to find Thomasin has returned home in the reddleman's van unmarried.

NOTES AND GLOSSARY:

Tartarean: Egdon is like the place of torture in Hades, the Greek underworld which is called Tartarus. It is a savage hell for the worst sinners
Amerigo Vespucci: Vespucci (1451–1512) claimed the honour of discovering America before Columbus, hence the name given to the two continents of America

Chapter 5: Perplexity among Honest People

Mrs Yeobright is haughty and domineering in her treatment of Thomasin. Wildeve enters the scene. 'Altogether he was one in whom no man would have seen anything to admire, and in whom no woman would have seen anything to dislike.' He is proud and clear-headed—a match for her. Even after the explanation of the confusion over the marriage licence she is not satisfied because she thinks it casts a slur on her family name. The rustics arrive to celebrate a wedding and they are not enlightened. They all notice again the bonfire still burning near Captain Vye's house. Wildeve is especially interested. It is a signal. He heads for the fire. What for?

NOTES AND GLOSSARY:

by my crown: by Christ

skimmity-riding: in country districts there was occasionally a procession accompanied by loud music in which husband or wife was held up to ridicule because of unfaithfulness or unkindness or some other reason

mead: an alcoholic drink made from honey

heling: pouring

club: a local benefit society

rozum: work away at

Farinelli: a famous Italian singer (Carlo Broschi, 1705–82) who delighted the Spanish court of Philip V

Sheridan's: the famous playwright Richard Brinsley Sheridan (1751–1816) spoke for six hours in charging Warren Hastings with appropriating funds from the begums (princesses) of Oude

tour de force: supreme achievement

gown-piece: cloth for making a dress

slittering: drifting aimlessly along

mossel: morsel

fess: Eustacia's bonfire is strong, vigorous

scattered: taken aback, confused, frightened

conceit: trick or fancy

biding: staying

Chapter 6: The Figure against the Sky

The mysterious figure of Eustacia Vye emerges on the heath. She is distracted or preoccupied and full of suppressed energy. (See the discussion of her in Part 3, page 52ff.) Johnny Nunsuch, who has been keeping her bonfire going, is to accompany Mrs Yeobright across the heath much later in the novel. The fire is a signal for Wildeve, and the splash of a stone in the pond a signal for Eustacia. They are still attracted to one another even though they fight for control of their relationship. He trifles with her and she teases him.

NOTES AND GLOSSARY:

Caesar: Caius Julius Caesar (102–44 BC) invaded Britain twice and was keen to move his troops out before the cold weather set in

Cimmerian land: where the sun never shines

Sappho: Greek poetess of Lesbos (*c*.650 BC) who drowned herself because a young man rejected her advances. The reader may take this into account when considering the circumstances of Eustacia's death

Mrs Siddons: a great tragic actress (1755–1831)

Belshazzar: while he, the last ruler of Babylon, was drinking from sacred cups stolen from Jerusalem, a hand appeared from nowhere to write the words of his doom on a wall

parian: fine white marble

Albertus Magnus: a scholar of the thirteenth century who is said to have made a brass statue chatter and move

crooked sixpence: supposed to chase away evil

Witch of Endor: she called up a figure from the dead who predicted the death of King Saul. Hardy's simile here is not particularly apt. It is far-fetched. The point is that Eustacia does have power over Wildeve, and to some characters in the novel she has witch-like qualities

Chapter 7: Queen of Night

This 'Queen of Night' chapter is one of the most memorable in *The Return of the Native*. Hardy gives a detailed and highly colourful analysis of his heroine. (See the discussion of Eustacia on page 52ff.)

NOTES AND GLOSSARY:

Olympus: the home of the gods in Greek mythology

distaff, spindle, shears: there were three Fates responsible for the birth, life, and death of men. The first sister Clotho held the distaff for the birth of man; Lachesis unwound the thread of man's life with a spindle; and Atropos cut the thread away with her shears. They were all-powerful

Ulex Europoeus: furze

ogee: an architectural term for two opposite curves that form a single line in the shape of the letter 'S'. Hardy becomes quite bemused by Eustacia's lips. She is of the earth and yet she is like a goddess

bourbon roses . . .: her presence conjures up romantic dreamy associations. In one mood she may, like the lotus-eaters, enjoy a drugged contentment; in another she may have the drive and vitality of the stirring march in *Athalie*. And she is like the Greek goddesses of old

Artemis, Athena, or Hera: Greek goddesses of the moon, of war and the queen of the heavens

Hades: hell

Tartarean: like the Titans she has been cast into Tartarus, a living hell. As a woman she has come from Budmouth to Egdon

Richter: Johann Paul Friedrich Richter (1763–1825), a German novelist

Corfiote: born on the island of Corfu

Alcinous: the generous and prosperous king of the Phaeacians in Homer's *Odyssey*

Phaeacia's isle: Corfu

Fitzalan and De Vere: by using these aristocratic names Hardy implies that she must be of noble birth to have such dignity

'a populous solitude': the quotation comes from Byron's *Childe Harold*

Saul, Sisera: violent leaders in the Bible who died tragically. Their deaths are described, respectively, in 2 Samuel 1, and Judges 4

Jacob, David: traditional, respected leaders. Eustacia prefers the romantic and nonconformist. It is a perverse streak in her nature that as a schoolgirl she took the side of the Philistines, the old enemies of the Jews in the Bible. She preferred bad characters to good. For example, Pontius Pilate, the Roman governor of Palestine at the time of Christ's crucifixion, attracted her attention more than did Christ

Delphian: the oracles at Delphi in Greece could be interpreted in two different ways

Héloïses: the love of Héloïse for Peter Abélard (1079–1142), the theologian, was noble and tragic

Cleopatras: the love of Cleopatra for Antony was selfish and consuming

Chapter 8: Those who are Found where there is said to be Nobody

On his way home from minding the fire Johnny is frightened by a dusty light and returns to Eustacia's fire. Hidden, he overhears the conversation of Eustacia and Wildeve. He is afraid to reveal himself and afraid to go home. He is faced with two evils like the sailors of old. Scylla was a sea-monster that terrified sailors. Charybdis was a dangerous whirlpool. 'Here was a Scyllaeo-Charybdean position for a poor boy.' He decides to head for home and he is discovered by the reddleman to whom he relates the lovers' conversation. The reddleman is intensely interested in their conversation. We wonder why. What is his interest? It is a habit of Hardy's to raise a question or to leave us in a state of suspense at the end of a chapter.

NOTES AND GLOSSARY:

tilt: a canvas covering over a cart

Chapter 9: Love leads a Shrewd Man into Strategy

Hardy gives the history and habits of reddlemen in general and a brief character sketch of this one in particular. He comes from a station in life higher than his present occupation, he would not be bad looking without his red colour, he is good-natured and acute. We learn that he had once proposed marriage to Thomasin and had been rejected. He still loves and wants to help her. That is why he stays on Egdon. He thinks that Eustacia is the reason for the non-marriage of Thomasin and Wildeve. We know that he is wrong. Diggory Venn sticks his nose into the business of other people. He spies on Eustacia and Wildeve, realises that they may continue to be lovers, and decides to go and see Eustacia.

NOTES AND GLOSSARY:

Mephistophelian: a devil who wore a red cloak

Arab: in this connection, nomadic

Cain: in the Bible, Cain killed his brother (Genesis 4:1–16). A mark was put on him so that everybody could recognise him. He walked alone for the rest of his life

ewe-lamb: a valuable possession

Tantalus: in Greek mythology, he betrayed the gods. As punishment he stood up to his neck in a river. Whenever he inclined his head to drink, the water receded. Above his head, just out of reach was a branch laden with fruit. Diggory Venn has a pessimistic outlook. He expects disappointment, suffering, and frustration. Life will tantalise him

Chapter 10: A Desperate Attempt at Persuasion

Venn pleads with Eustacia to give up Wildeve so that his marriage with Thomasin may proceed. His arguments are unsuccessful. Because another woman wants Wildeve, Eustacia wants him all the more.

NOTES AND GLOSSARY:

Aegean: the Aegean Sea in which small islands abound

bustard: a large bird

marsh-harriers: falcons

courser: a long-legged bird

mallard: wild duck

Franklin: Sir John Franklin (1786–1847), an Arctic explorer who disappeared

cotter: farm labourer

grog: a mixture of spirits, hot water, lemon, and sugar

withywind: a weed that twines itself around other plants

Candaules' wife: he allowed a shepherd to see his wife unveiled. Furious, she persuaded the shepherd to kill her husband, then married him. The story is in Herodotus (*c*.484–420 BC), the Greek historian

a Carthaginian . . .: in the imaginations of the heath-folk Budmouth consists of numerous buildings, rich and self-indulgent inhabitants, and is a health resort

Zenobia: princess (3rd century AD) of a city in the Syrian desert. She killed her husband Odenathus, and tried to extend her kingdom, aiming at independence from Rome. She did not care what the Romans thought of her; she was finally captured and lived near Tivoli

Chapter 11: The Dishonesty of an Honest Woman

Mrs Yeobright makes Wildeve believe that another man wants to marry Thomasin and that she can persuade her to accept him. Mrs Yeobright really wants Wildeve to hurry up and marry Thomasin. Wildeve goes to Eustacia and gives her a week to make up her mind to marry him or not. Eustacia now realises that she no longer wants him because she thinks he has been rejected by another woman. The first book, 'The Three Women', ends with the news that Clym Yeobright is coming home for Christmas.

BOOK SECOND: THE ARRIVAL

Chapter 1: Tidings of the Comer

As Humphrey and Sam make piles of the furze they have cut they discuss Clym Yeobright and suggest that he would make a good match with Eustacia, who overhears their conversation. She fires her imagination with visions of an exciting young man from Paris. They also discuss

Thomasin and Wildeve. The locals focus our attention on the centre of the novel—the return of the native. They introduce him, and, like Eustacia, the reader is keen to meet him.

NOTES AND GLOSSARY:

Adam: the first man on earth

mind: remember

scroff: dirt

'Castle of Indolence': Eustacia, like the people in the poem by James Thomson (1700–48), is aroused from her boredom

Chapter 2: The People at Blooms-End make ready

Thomasin and Mrs Yeobright gather apples, berries, and mistletoe and make other preparations for Clym's arrival. Thomasin does not want Clym to know about the bungled marriage. Mrs Yeobright promises to tell her later why she told Wildeve that somebody else wanted to marry her.

NOTES AND GLOSSARY:

russets . . . ribstones: types of apple

stratum of ensaffroned light: layer of orange-red

Chapter 3: How a Little Sound produced a Great Dream

In the dark a male voice bids Eustacia 'Goodnight!'. She believes that she was meant to meet Clym that night and she cannot understand why somebody should choose to come to Egdon from Paris. Eustacia dreams of her knight in shining armour, falls in love with her own picture or vision of him, and goes for walks hoping to meet him.

NOTES AND GLOSSARY:

Dr Kitto: an English scholar (1804–54) who fell off a roof, became deaf, and wrote a book called *The Lost Senses*

Nebuchadnezzar . . . Swaffham tinker: Nebuchadnezzar, King of Babylonia (604–561 BC), and the Swaffham pedlar had remarkable dreams (like Eustacia). Hardy's allusions here are not strictly necessary because they add nothing to the meaning

Cretan labyrinth: it is a complicated dream like the famous mythological maze in Crete where the Minotaur, half-man half-bull, lived

parterre: flower-garden

Scheherazade: a legendary figure in the *Arabian Nights* who specialised in relating fantastic stories to the Caliph Haroun al Rashid
circumambulated: walked around

Chapter 4: Eustacia is led on to an Adventure

The mummers rehearse *Saint George* in the fuel-house as Eustacia looks on. On hearing that their first performance is to be at Mrs Yeobright's party, Eustacia arranges to play Charley's part so that she can go. As a reward Charley is allowed to hold her bare hand. It looks as though Clym and Eustacia will meet yet. Eustacia realises that 'want of an object to live for—that's all is the matter with me!' She makes Clym that object.

NOTES AND GLOSSARY:
Tussaud . . .: they look like wax figures in the Museum of Waxworks established in London by Madame Tussaud (1760–1850)
mummers: actors
Balaam: this allusion to Balaam, a prophet in the Bible who disobeyed God by cursing the Israelites, (Numbers 22) is also inappropriate in attempting to describe how children approach their parts in a play
the well known play of 'Saint George': a folk play in which the patron saint of England fights the Saracens at the time of the Crusades
unweeting: unthinking
gorget . . .: armour for various parts of the body
guisers: actors
Raffaelle . . .: just as Raffaelle (Raphael Santi, or Raffaello Sanzio 1483–1520) was a better artist than Perugino (Pietro Vannucci 1481–1537), so Eustacia is a better performer than Charley

Chapter 5: Through the Moonlight

The actors play their parts, Eustacia falls dead. Now she can look around to find Clym who she hopes is a 'sufficient hero'.

NOTES AND GLOSSARY:
serpent: a bass wind-instrument

Chapter 6: The Two stand Face to Face

At last she sees him. Although she could see all of him she was conscious only of his face which reflected the intensity of his experience. Hardy expounds one of his favourite theories here—that thought is a disease of the flesh. (For a discussion of Clym see Part 3, page 49ff.) Eustacia finds his presence disturbing. Dressed as a boy she cannot display her charms and fears that Clym may take a liking to Thomasin. Beside the palings under the moon Eustacia and Clym have a brief conversation which gives her a new lease of life. She sighs one of her tragic sighs and wishes that Wildeve and Thomasin were married.

NOTES AND GLOSSARY:

Rembrandt:	Rembrandt van Rijn (1606–69) liked to highlight faces with strong light in his paintings
Jared . . .:	men who lived for hundreds of years
scammish:	untidy
bagnet:	bayonet
spatterdashes:	leggings
shadder:	shadow
Queen, love . . .:	In Virgil's *Aeneid* Venus, disguised as a huntress, appeared to her son Aeneas. Eustacia felt like the mountain nymph who was changed into an echo because her physical qualities are concealed and all she has is a voice
Polly Peachum:	the first actress to play this part in *The Beggar's Opera* (1728) by John Gay (1685–1732) was made a duchess
Lydia Languish:	an actress who played this part in Sheridan's *The Rivals* (1775) in the nineteenth century was made a duchess

Chapter 7: A Coalition between Beauty and Oddness

Eustacia now realises that Mrs Yeobright had mentioned another lover in order to hasten Wildeve's marriage to Thomasin. The reddleman is surprised to hear from her that she is keen to hasten it too. She vows to break her relationship with Wildeve and Venn offers to deliver some things from her to him. When Wildeve reads her letter he is afraid he might lose Thomasin also and hastens to her house to propose marriage. Another reason is that he wants to spite Eustacia. Nobody yet knows that Eustacia wants Clym.

NOTES AND GLOSSARY:

pis aller:	(*French*) a last resort, for want of anything better

bucks: gay young fellows. Today a 'buck-party' is a party for men only

Ahasuerus: a mythical figure, the Wandering Jew was condemned to walk the earth until Christ's second coming

Israel: people can't understand why Venn stays in Egdon just as the Israelites couldn't understand why Moses wanted them to stay in the wilderness of Zin

Ishmaelitish: outcast. Ishmael, oldest son of Abraham and Hagar, became founder of the Ishmaelites. He was banished to the wilderness. His story is told in the Bible (Genesis 16:12 and 21:14)

serpenting: winding his way like a serpent or a snake

Ithuriel's spear: when the angel Ithuriel in Milton's *Paradise Lost* (1667) touches Satan, disguised as a toad, with his spear, Satan assumes his proper shape

Chapter 8: Firmness is discovered in a Gentle Heart

Thomasin feels it her duty to marry Wildeve. She still loves him but does not think, as she used to, that he is the perfect man. Mrs Yeobright and she have avoided the public eye. They have felt ashamed because of the confusion over the marriage. And it has caused Clym distress as we can see from his letter. The feeling is that the wedding will make everybody much happier. The reader cannot help wishing that Mrs Yeobright would mind her own business.

Eustacia gives Thomasin away. As she signs the register Wildeve looks at Eustacia with triumph. 'This will teach you' is what his glance expresses. She quietly replies that she is delighted to see him married.

After the wedding the reddleman leaves Egdon. There appears to be nothing left for him to do.

BOOK THIRD: THE FASCINATION

Chapter 1: 'My Mind to me a Kingdom is'

This is a key chapter in any discussion of Clym Yeobright. His face reflects a new age, a new way of looking at life. He does not love life. He sees it as something to be put up with. As a boy he was precocious: great things were expected of him. As a boy he was very much part of Egdon. A neighbour sent him to Budmouth on the death of his father. From there he went to London, then to Paris as manager to a diamond merchant. Clym explains to the locals during the Sunday hair-cutting ceremony that he has come home to stay. The reasons he gives are:

(1) the diamond trade is pointless and effeminate
(2) he wants to serve his own people on Egdon
(3) he wants to run a night-school

The plot takes an ominous turn here. We are being prepared for failure or disaster. 'He'll never carry it out in the world' said Fairway. Another man describes him as 'good-hearted' but thinks 'he had better mind his business'. The locals speak the truth in this novel.

NOTES AND GLOSSARY:

Pheidias: a great sculptor (*c*.490–432 BC) who supervised the construction of the Parthenon at Athens, his masterpiece being a figure of Zeus at Olympia. Fragments of his work are among the Elgin Marbles in the British Museum, London

. . . a long line of . . .: time has removed any illusions we may have had about life

Aeschylus: Greek tragedian (525–456 BC), who wrote about seventy dramas of which seven survive

Gracian: Baltasar Gracian y Morales (1601–58), a Spanish churchman

Homer: ancient Greek epic poet (probably lived between 1100–900 BC) who according to tradition wrote the *Iliad* and the *Odyssey*

Clive: Robert Clive, Baron Clive of Plassey, (1725–74) went to India in the service of the East India Company; he established British supremacy in Bengal and can be regarded as initially the founder of the British Empire in India

Gay: playwright (1685–1732), author of *The Beggar's Opera*; his fables were famous

Keats: John Keats, English romantic poet (1795–1821). Once again these references are pointless because Clym Yeobright has nothing in common with Gay, Clive, or Keats. All the paragraph means is that Clym started on a career by chance

bide: stay

mollyhorning: mucking, playing

Chapter 2: The New Course causes Disappointment

Hardy analyses Clym's mind and intentions. Clym explains to his mother why he cannot go back to Paris. She is very disappointed.

Christian Cantle brings news that Susan Nunsuch pricked Eustacia with a needle in church. Clym's interest in Eustacia is aroused by Sam's account of her. He wonders if she was the disguised mummer, and wonders if she would like to teach.

NOTES AND GLOSSARY:

bucolic:	rural, country
We can . . .:	there is no point in preaching the values of an intellectual life to somebody who enjoys the country life if you don't provide him with material benefits too
John the Baptist:	went ahead of Christ and asked people to repent
Had Philip's . . .:	an unnecessary and inept illustration of the previous sentence. The same applies to the comparison referring to the Chaldeans in the next paragraph and to the references to Rogers, West, North, Tomline. It does not really matter if you know who they are or not
eremites:	hermits
plashed hedges:	hedges with branches interlacing to form neat fences
rum:	strange

Chapter 3: The First Act in a Timeworn Drama

Clym helps the men to retrieve the bucket from Captain Vye's well and discovers that Eustacia was the disguised mummer. They are mutually attracted even though he loves the heath and she hates it. Eustacia feels that her life has just started. Mrs Yeobright thinks that Clym's life has just ended, that he is making a dreadful mistake in falling in love with an idle hussy. The lovers share a kiss; mother and son share friction. Hardy discusses the character of Mrs Yeobright in depth.

NOTES AND GLOSSARY:

fieldfare:	a thrush
helical:	spiral
sommat:	something
crotchets:	whims, fancies
Blacklock:	Thomas Blacklock (1721–91), a Scottish poet
Sanderson:	Nicholas Sanderson (1682–1739), a skilled blind lecturer on optics and other things
Sallaert, van Alsloot:	Antonius Sallaert (*c.*1590–1657) and Denis van Alsloot (1570–1626), painters born in Brussels. Like them, Mrs Yeobright looks at people and society from a distance

Chapter 4: An Hour of Bliss and many Hours of Sadness

The lovers embrace under an eclipse of the moon. Their conversation is stilted. They sound like lovers playing at being tragic figures on the stage of Egdon. Whenever he wants to talk about marriage she wants to talk about Paris. The plot thickens and becomes more ominous. Seeds of discontent and discord are sown already because Clym knows 'that she loved him rather as a visitant from a gay world to which she rightly belonged than as a man with a purpose opposed to that recent past of his which so interested her'.

She does not think that Clym will pursue his education plan and agrees to marry him although she doubts that she will make a good wife. He fears that he cannot please his mother and make Eustacia happy too. Apprehension, rather than joy, is the keynote of this chapter.

NOTES AND GLOSSARY:

Tuileries: used to be a royal palace in Paris
Louvre: the famous French art gallery in Paris
Versailles: a palace outside Paris
Trianon: a small palace in Versailles
Fontainebleau: palaces and gardens outside Paris
Petrarch: Italian lyric poet (1304–74), wrote a series of love-poems to Laura, wife of an Italian noble

Chapter 5: Sharp Words are Spoken, and a Crisis Ensues

Mrs Yeobright objects to Clym's marriage because Eustacia is idle and voluptuous and because she is a Corfu bandmaster's daughter. She also thinks his ideas about education absurd. Clym decides to leave home. The lovers agree to marry in a fortnight and to live in a cottage for no more than six months before moving to Budmouth 'if no misfortune happens'. We already expect it.

NOTES AND GLOSSARY:

carboniferous period: 300 million years ago
carpe diem: (*Latin*) enjoy yourself while you can

Chapter 6: Yeobright goes, and the Breach is complete

Clym arranges to buy a cottage, comes home wet and weary, and bids his mother farewell. Thomasin visits her aunt because her husband will not give her any money. Mrs Yeobright mentions a small inheritance she may have but wants Thomasin to ask her husband for money first. Thomasin tries to console her because she feels rejected by her son. It is a tearful and somewhat tiresome scene. When Wildeve hears of the marriage he wants Eustacia again just because another man wants her.

NOTES AND GLOSSARY:

mart: shopping centre

spade-guineas: the shield on the coin was shaped like a spade

Ulysses: the hero of Homer's *Odyssey*, who experienced many adventures in ten years of wandering before returning home after the siege of Troy

stun-poll: Charley is stunned like a fool by Eustacia's beauty

Rousseau: Wildeve leads an erratic existence. That is all he has in common with Jean Jacques Rousseau (1712–78) whose *Confessions* shed light on his irregular life. Hardy means that Wildeve has fanciful and romantic notions

Chapter 7: The Morning and the Evening of a Day

Mrs Yeobright broods over the marriage and sends the guineas for Thomasin and Clym with Christian Cantle, who is talked into a raffle at The Quiet Woman and wins. The reddleman watches from a corner. Led on by Wildeve who tells him stories of men losing everything then winning everything, Christian plays dice with Wildeve on the heath and loses all the guineas. Then the reddleman confronts the startled Wildeve.

NOTES AND GLOSSARY:

rue: regret

impolitic: unwise

Pitt Diamond: Thomas Pitt (1653–1726), governor of Madras and a businessman, sent the diamond hidden in a shoe from India to England

gown-piece: cloth for a garment

raffle: game played with three dice in which the highest score is three of a kind or pair-royal, such as three fours, three sixes . . .

cudgel-playing: a fight with heavy sticks

black art: magic

ba'dy gaieties: bawdy, spicy stories, indecent remarks

pedlar: a travelling salesman, packman, chapman

born w' a caul: that is, born lucky

pot-boy: somebody who serves drinks

jambs: sides

niche: corner
nick-nack: ornament
chips-in-porridge: harmless, useless fellow

Chapter 8: A New Force disturbs the Current

By the light of glowworms, watched by wild ponies, Venn beats Wildeve at dice and gives all the money to Thomasin. Venn, thinking he is being very helpful and kind, makes matters much worse by his interference because he does not know that half the money was for Clym. Wildeve sees the newly-weds and yearns for Eustacia.

NOTES AND GLOSSARY:
Arab: Hardy thinks that Arabs possess dignity, and an ability to sit perfectly still
diorama . . .: their eyes mirrored the ups and downs of the game. A diorama is a spectacular painting from which varied effects are got by throwing coloured lights on and through it
heath-croppers: small wild ponies

BOOK FOURTH: THE CLOSED DOOR

Chapter 1: The Rencounter by the Pool

The lovers spend three or four weeks in their cottage in happiness and contentment. Clym studies hard. Mrs Yeobright, wondering why she has not received a note of thanks from her son for the money, goes to see Eustacia who is visiting her grandfather at Mistover. Thinking that Wildeve won all the money as Christian told her, she asks Eustacia if Wildeve gave her a gift of money; thinking that Mrs Yeobright knows of her intimate relations with Wildeve, Eustacia interprets the question as an affront to her dignity and honour. The argument is bitter, each woman standing on her pride and self-righteousness. She warns Eustacia that Clym can be 'as hard as steel'. The plot moves on, a further strand is about to be woven.

NOTES AND GLOSSARY:
gied: given

Chapter 2: He is set upon by Adversities; but he sings a Song

The immediate result of the argument is that Eustacia asks Clym to take her away from Egdon to Paris. He refuses and resolves to study even harder. This results in temporary blindness or acute inflammation of the eyes. Eustacia cries in the garden: no Paris, and now this. To earn some money Clym works as a turf-cutter. It is too much for her. Eustacia is horrified that Clym should adopt the humblest of occupations. Clym is completely at home in his new job with bees, butterflies, grasshoppers, flies, snakes, and rabbits as his companions. He feels that he is part of the heath; he belongs there. After two months her love for him has cooled because she sees him as a social failure degrading himself.

NOTES AND GLOSSARY:

excoriating: tears so hot that they seem to strip or burn the skin

stoic: one who endures hardship with courage

'Rasselas': in this novel by Samuel Johnson (1709–84) a man tries to fly without success by attaching to himself wings which manage to keep him afloat in the lake into which he falls

'Le point du jour': (*French*) a song about daybreak and the pain it causes the shepherd in having to leave his loved one

Chapter 3: She goes out to Battle against Depression

To shake off her depression Eustacia dances with Wildeve at the village festivities. He is in his element dancing with another man's wife and he sympathises with Eustacia's fate. As he walks her part of the way home they see Clym and Venn approaching. They part. Venn hastens to the inn to see if Wildeve is there. His suspicions are confirmed. It was Wildeve he saw with Eustacia. Thomasin tells him that her husband went to buy a horse. Venn tells her that he saw him leading one home—'A beauty, with a white face and a mane as black as night'. She tells Wildeve, who realises that Venn is sticking his nose into his affairs again.

NOTES AND GLOSSARY:

wideawake: type of hat

Chapter 4: Rough Coercion is Employed

Venn excels himself as a busybody. To discourage Wildeve from going near Eustacia's house he trips him up on the heath, knocks at Eustacia's door while Wildeve waits by a window, and later fires a gun at him. He informs Mrs Yeobright of the renewed friendship between the two main figures in the novel and persuades her to visit her son. His action will have a tragic outcome. There is further tragic irony in the fact that Clym is resolved to visit his mother to heal the breach. Her journey, then, is not really necessary. Eustacia's feeling is that had the native never returned to Egdon it would have been a good thing for Clym and four other people.

NOTES AND GLOSSARY:

coup-de-Jarnac: (*French*) an underhand attack

Farmer Lynch's: many triumphs of justice are achieved by illegal and underhand means such as those adopted by Charles Lynch (1736–96), an American justice whose name gave us the word 'lynching'; he punished people without trial

Chapter 5: The Journey across the Heath

In stifling heat Mrs Yeobright crosses the heath with great difficulty to her son's house. Unaware that she is following him and unaware that she is horrified to see him in the garb of a furze-cutter, Clym reaches home and throws down his hook and faggots at the door. That is the last time she will see her son. Things do not look well for the weary woman resting under the battered trees.

NOTES AND GLOSSARY:

sapphirine: blue like a sapphire

ephemerons: insects

Ahimaaz: in the Bible (2 Samuel 17:19–28) he was a messenger to King David, recognised from a distance by his manner of running

abject: helpless, despicable

Shakespeare etc.: places of historic interest

Chapter 6: A Conjuncture, and its Result upon the Pedestrian

Wildeve and Eustacia discuss their lives. She is unhappy, unlucky. She wants 'music, poetry, passion, war'. However if Clym can sing happily to himself at work she will force herself to shake off depression. Clym lies asleep on the floor as they talk. Wildeve wants Eustacia again but she makes it clear that even though they have been 'hot lovers' in the past, that is not possible now, and she asks him not to call again. Unaware, Clym sleeps on. As they talk Mrs Yeobright knocks at the door. Eustacia does not open the door. They retreat by the back door to the garden because she has heard Clym say 'Mother' and assumes he will open the door. Unaware, Clym sleeps on, talking in his sleep.

Mrs Yeobright stumbles forlorn and rejected back across the heath with Johnny Nunsuch. It so happens that the path she chooses cannot be seen by Eustacia who has found Clym still asleep and who has looked out of the door to find nobody there. Mrs Yeobright cannot forget

Clym's hook at the door and Eustacia's face at the window. She is 'a broken-hearted woman cast off by her son'. Hardy makes her a pathetic figure despite his melodramatic methods.

NOTES AND GLOSSARY:

marnels:	marbles
reticule:	a small bag
ooser:	a frightening mask

Chapter 7: The Tragic Meeting of Two Old Friends

It so happens that Clym has been dreaming that he and Eustacia went to his mother's house but couldn't get in while she was crying out for help. This is a good example of a melodramatic method. Not knowing what to say about his mother's visit, Eustacia says nothing. In the evening Clym leaves to see his mother and finds her dying on the heath. He feels like a small boy back on the heath with his mother, and he is distraught because he does not know what she is doing there. He carries her to a hut; the locals arrive. They try to restore her with brandy and use some folk medicine to cure the bite of the adder.

NOTES AND GLOSSARY:

Aeneas:	as Clym carries his mother across the heath Hardy compares him with Virgil's Aeneas carrying his father out of burning Troy

Chapter 8: Eustacia hears of Good Fortune, and beholds Evil

Meanwhile Eustacia blames some vague fate for what happened. She learns of Wildeve's inheritance and goes for a walk with him. They happen to come across the hut where Mrs Yeobright dies. The final blow to Clym is the message delivered by Johnny Nunsuch: 'and she said I was to say that I had seed her, and she was a broken-hearted woman and cast off by her son'.

NOTES AND GLOSSARY:

overlooked:	given the evil eye
purblind:	half-blind

BOOK FIFTH: THE DISCOVERY

Chapter 1: 'Wherefore is Light given to him that is in Misery?'

Prostrated by anguish and remorse Clym has been very ill for about two weeks. His existence is like a nightmare. He curses himself and wishes himself in hell as he broods over his mother's death and the words of Johnny Nunsuch. The death of a mother is bad enough but he thinks he caused it. She was cast out like a dog to die alone, thinking that he had rejected her. He, who was going 'to teach people the higher secrets of happiness', could not even look after his own mother. For two and a half months his mother had lived alone grieving the loss of a son who lived only six miles away and who did not bother to visit her. Clym tortures himself endlessly. Eustacia remains afraid to tell him of his mother's visit. She fears the fury of a patient man. When Wildeve arrives he suggests that Eustacia should never tell Clym that he was in the house with her when Mrs Yeobright called.

NOTES AND GLOSSARY:

Judas Iscariot: one of the disciples who betrayed Christ, and later hanged himself. Eustacia is haunted by the ghost of a worn-out woman knocking at a door

Black Hole: one hundred and forty-six British people were thrown into a punishment cell in Calcutta in 1756 during the Indian mutiny and only twenty-three were alive the next day

Chapter 2: A Lurid Light breaks in upon a Darkened Understanding

Clym's grief exhausts itself. Christian Cantle tells him that Mrs Yeobright was going to see him that day and that Venn knows why she went. Clym is very surprised. It so happens that Venn left the heath the day after and does not know about his mother's death. Venn assures him that his mother forgave him. Clym, unable to see why his mother later blamed him, goes to find out more from Johnny Nunsuch. He learns of the male visitor, of Eustacia's face at the window, and of his mother's turning back. Clym cannot reach the heights of a tragic figure because Egdon reduces him to insignificance, but this does not ease his suffering.

NOTES AND GLOSSARY:

mitigated: less strong

equanimity: of even mind, neither happy nor depressed

taciturnity: silence

spudding: digging

twanky: annoyed

Ascension: of Christ, a reference to his ascendance from earth into heaven

Miraculous draught of fishes: one of Christ's miracles

carking: wearing down, irritating

gleaning: learning
enigma: riddle, puzzle
insuavity: lack of politeness
Oedipus: in Greek legend when Oedipus learned that he had killed his father and married his mother he tore his eyes out. When Clym thinks of Eustacia as a murderess his face reflects the anguish of Oedipus

Chapter 3: Eustacia dresses herself on a Black Morning

In a rage he confronts Eustacia with her guilt. She resents his manner because her only fault was that she did not open the door after the first knock. This scene destroys their love. Words are said that cannot be unsaid. He accuses her of being a harlot and she does not like that. He rifles her desk in his search for a lover's letter. Clym now means nothing to her and she leaves after telling him of his mother's visit. It is a touching moment when he helps tie the strings of her bonnet.

NOTES AND GLOSSARY:

impassivity . . .: Clym feels that no matter what he experiences, the heath will remain imperturbable, cool, unsympathetic
superstratum: surface layer
adept: prostitute
hind: a poor rustic

Chapter 4: The Ministrations of a Half-Forgotten One

When Charley beholds the romantic vision of Eustacia in such a helpless, indifferent, wild state quite oblivious to her surroundings, he is all attention in providing fires and food and in dancing attendance on her. She thinks of killing herself. Charley sees her looking at a pair of pistols. He hides them. Her grandfather asks no questions. It is clear that she has lost interest in living.

Chapter 5: An Old Move inadvertently repeated

A week passes. Eustacia stays in her grandfather's house. The fifth of November has come round again and Charley makes a bonfire to please and surprise her. Naturally enough Wildeve takes it as a signal, comes to see her, and offers any help she wants to relieve her distress. She asks him to take her to Budmouth where she can get a boat to France. She will signal him. Eustacia has to decide whether Wildeve remains a friend or becomes a lover again.

Chapter 6: Thomasin argues with her Cousin, and he writes a Letter

Clym, just as miserable, wishes she would come back to him. After writing a letter begging her to return, he makes up his mind to wait until the evening of the next day before sending it. Perhaps she will turn up anyway. Of course if he had sent the letter straight away the outcome of the novel would have been quite different. His gesture is to be too late. Hardy draws a brief contrast again between Eustacia who hates the heath and Thomasin who admires 'its grim old face'.

Chapter 7: The Night of the Sixth of November

It is November the sixth. A year and a day have passed since the novel started. There is a stormy wind and rain threatens. Eustacia, who used to think of Egdon as a prison, and now thinks of the world as an unpleasant place, prepares to leave. She signals to Wildeve who is to meet her at midnight. Eustacia lies down to rest, Fairway delivers Clym's letter and Captain Vye brings it to her room. Thinking she is asleep he takes it downstairs and leaves it on the mantlepiece in the parlour. Later he hears her crying as she passes his door to go out. 'Even the receipt of Clym's letter would not have stopped her now.' The night feels like a funeral. The chaos of her mind and of the world harmonise well. Her tears join the rain. 'The cruel obstructiveness of all about her' has destroyed her soul. She would not feel any happier even if she got to Budmouth. She has no money to go alone; she will not break her marriage vow and go with Wildeve. That is her dilemma. There really is no point in going on living. She blames forces beyond her control for her unhappy fate.

While she shouts to the heath, her waxen image melts in the fire of Susan Nunsuch.

NOTES AND GLOSSARY:

posset: a drink for a cold

the last plague of Egypt: in the Bible, all the first-born of the Egyptians died as a punishment from God (Exodus 12:29)

Sennacherib's host: field-mice ate the bow-strings of the army of Sennacherib, King of Assyria, in the night, and his men were powerless. The biblical reference is 2 Kings 19:35

Gethsemane: the garden where Christ spent his last night before he was betrayed by Judas Iscariot

lugubrious: mournful

Chapter 8: Rain, Darkness and Anxious Wanderers

The storm grows worse as the evening advances. Clym hopes that Eustacia will come to him. Thomasin tells him that Damon and Eustacia are going to run away together and asks him to help her to prevent this. Clym makes his way through the rain to The Quiet Woman to be followed by Thomasin struggling through the heath with her baby. Venn offers to guide her home. He heard a woman crying on the heath earlier.

NOTES AND GLOSSARY:

peregrination:	journey
Saint Sebastian:	a third century AD Christian martyr shot to death with arrows
quag:	bog

Chapter 9: Sights and Sounds draw the Wanderers Together

Venn waits for Eustacia with his horse and gig. Clym comes across him at a quarter past midnight. Eustacia is late. They hear the sound of a body falling into the pool at Shadwater Weir and rush to the rescue. Their attempts to save her from drowning are futile. Wildeve drowns; Yeobright survives. He considers himself responsible for the deaths of Eustacia and his mother.

NOTES AND GLOSSARY:

packet:	boat
hartshorn:	ammonia
Lazarus:	brother of Mary and Martha whom Christ raised from the dead. The biblical reference is to John 11

BOOK SIXTH: AFTERCOURSES

Chapter 1: The Inevitable Movement Onward

Because nobody blames Clym he blames himself all the more bitterly. 'It might have been said that he had a wrinkled mind.' A year passes. Venn returns without his reddle after buying his father's dairy. We know what he is after. After the Maypole celebrations he looks for a lady's lost glove. We know that they are going to live happily ever after.

NOTES AND GLOSSARY:

First Cause:	God
diaphanous:	transparent

Babylon: a reference to the Babylonish captivity of the Jews who lived by the river in Mesopotamia, today's Iraq. This paragraph is a good example of the way in which Hardy sometimes intrudes to deliver a message or sermon. He interrupts the narrative unnecessarily to talk about issues that do not contribute to the development of the plot, such as it is, in 'Aftercourses'

Chapter 2: Thomasin walks in a Green Place by the Roman Road

Thomasin cannot work out which woman has taken Venn's fancy until he returns her glove.

Chapter 3: The Serious Discourse of Clym with his Cousin

Clym doesn't think he should marry Thomasin because his passion is spent; he visits cemeteries, and is preparing to be a preacher. He is right.

NOTES AND GLOSSARY:

fiat: instruction

eleventh commandment: there were ten commandments; Hardy implies that the eleventh commandment is 'love thy neighbour'

Chapter 4: Cheerfulness again asserts itself at Blooms-End, and Clym finds his Vocation

The rustics discuss the marriage and prepare a present. During the wedding party Clym prepares a sermon and gives Charley a lock of Eustacia's hair. He seems to be so sorry for himself that he thinks the guests are drinking his health and not that of the newly-weds. Clym stands alone at the end preaching to the country people on Rainbarrow.

NOTES AND GLOSSARY:

coterie: group

bed-tick: cover of a mattress

a bruckle hit: a poor shot

maul: grab

And the king . . .: in the Bible Solomon the king did not grant Bathsheba his mother her request (1 Kings 2:19–20). She wanted an enemy of Solomon to be allowed to marry whom he chose. Perhaps Clym chooses this text because he did not follow his mother's advice

Part 3

Commentary

The Return of the Native is about a young man who returns to his place of birth to pursue an impossible ideal. In his pursuit he happens to be the indirect cause of the deaths of his mother, wife, and cousin's husband. At the end he finds his vocation as a preacher. On the barrow he is probably a more pathetic, lonely figure than his wife had been at the beginning of the novel. Hardy does not say that Clym Yeobright is better or worse off at the end of the novel. He leaves it to the reader to form his own impressions. Clym is certainly better off than Eustacia who is dead. Hardy shows us what to look at but not how to look at it. He believed that a novel was an impression not an argument. A novel, then, is a piece of life, and not an attempt to show what life is or should be about.

Eustacia is the most fascinating person in the novel. Compared with her, Clym is dull, insipid, colourless. *The Return of the Native* is also about a young woman with an impossible aim—'to be loved to madness'. She is in love with the idea of love as a means of escaping from her boredom and loneliness. When she first met Wildeve she created an imaginary picture of him in her mind's eye and fell in love with that for a while; even before she met Clym she imagined him as a knight in shining armour and decided to fall in love with that. 'And she seemed to long for the abstraction called passionate love more than for any particular lover.' Her death is accident or suicide. And again Hardy leaves it to the reader to form his own impression.

The Return of the Native is set in Wessex, a small area of land in the south of England. The action of the novel takes place on Egdon Heath. The time of the action from Book First to the end of Book Fifth is a year and a day. Because Hardy's Wessex is such a small area the reader often has a feeling that characters keep bumping into one another, or seeing one another out of windows or over hedges, or following one another, or overhearing one another. This is a characteristic of Hardy's regional novels. We are in a small world that is claustrophobic and old-fashioned. Often too, things seem to happen by chance. Coincidence is inevitable in such a tiny world. And anyway it is part of Hardy's narrative technique. Things that happen by chance are necessary to his novels. He believed that any story worth telling should be unusual enough to grip the reader and that the unusualness should be in the events rather than the characters. So Clym happens to be asleep when his mother knocks at the door; so Clym's letter to Eustacia happens to be left above the fireplace; so the reddleman reappears at The Quiet Woman in time to follow Wildeve to a game of dice on the heath; and so on.

In his Preface to the Wessex Edition of 1912 Hardy says that the action of Greek plays was enacted in an area of land not much larger than Wessex and that Wessex is big enough for his purposes because 'domestic emotions have throbbed in Wessex nooks with as much intensity as in the places of Europe'. Hardy recreates the landscape of Wessex in painstaking, accurate detail. The people who live on it live as they have done for centuries gathering furze, lighting bonfires, dancing around the Maypole, drinking at the inn, oiling their boots, telling stories, exchanging jokes and fears and superstitions, and sleeping in peace. The rustics in Hardy's novels are part of the anonymous rural landscape. They reflect Egdon because they are Egdon. This history of Wessex, customs, architecture, prehistoric antiquities, and folk-lore help to create the overall atmosphere or mood of this novel.

There is a strong feeling in the novel that things will not change. What has been, is now, and will continue. Ways of living and doing things will continue no matter how hard a Clym Yeobright wants to change them, no matter how hard a Eustacia Vye tries to resist and escape from them. Landscape, history, architecture, customs will remain; people will not. That is why the atmosphere of the novel is heavy and oppressive despite attempts at jokes from the rustics. The barrow on which Clym and Eustacia stood and embraced under an eclipse of the moon remains.

All these things express Hardy's point of view. At one moment he will describe the rustics lighting bonfires, at the next he will be reflecting on the historical significance of fire; at one moment he will describe the splash of a stone in a pond, and soon after he will talk about fate or destiny. Such shifts in attention are essential to his purpose and they help to make the plot, however skilfully contrived, slow moving. The pace of the novel is slow and deliberate. There is something solemn and inevitable about the development of the plot. It is almost as though he treats his characters as sad objects on the way to the graveyard.

An air of melancholy then, hangs over the novel. Hardy's prose style creates it too. If you look closely at the first few pages of the novel you will find a prose style that is formal and stiff. Your first impression might have been that the words are strange and old-fashioned. Sentences are long and are constructed in a deliberate, precise way. His style suits his theme. And however irritated you may become by the number of classical, biblical, historical, and literary allusions, these too suit his theme and help to enrich the texture of the novel. They make the cake richer. There is, of course, the occasional unnecessary ingredient that makes it a bit stodgy.

The characters themselves create a sense of gloom, if not futility. Near the beginning Christian Cantle says: '’Twas to be if ’twas, I suppose.' There is nothing that he or anybody else could have done to have prevented his speaking about marriage. Olly Dowden says to Mrs Yeobright: 'What's done cannot be undone.' Such local sayings suggest a fate or destiny beyond human control. What is meant to be will be. As Clym says with resignation, 'Well, what must be will be.' The feeling of the characters is that there is a controlling order which is out to beat them. Their attitude is negative. Hardy does not comment on their views. He simply allows them to express their feelings. Eustacia feels that destiny has been against her; the reddleman, that man is doomed to disappointment; Clym, that 'men are born to misery' and that the general human situation is grim.

Although Hardy does not comment on their views we often feel that characters are expressing the views of Hardy. This is particularly true of the character sketch of Clym in Book Second, Chapter 6. There are times when Hardy does not allow a character to exist, to grow, to develop. There are times when he tells us all there is to know about the character. Rather than show us a character in action, he tells us what to expect of him. In this particular case Hardy wants to make the point that 'thought is a disease of the flesh'. It is an idea he developed in later novels such as *Jude the Obscure* in which consciousness means death. People who live without thinking about it do well in Hardy's world. Those who think, and try to change the way of life into which they were born, suffer and often die.

Hardy is trying to present his idea of modern man in Clym Yeobright:

> In Clym Yeobright's face could be dimly seen the typical countenance of the future. Should there be a classic period to art hereafter, its Pheidias may produce such faces. The view of life as a thing to be put up with, replacing that zest for existence which was so intense in early civilisations, must ultimately enter so thoroughly into the constitution of the advanced races that its facial expression will become accepted as a new artistic departure. People already feel that a man who lives without disturbing a curve of feature, or setting a mark of mental concern anywhere upon himself, is too far removed from modern perceptiveness to be a modern type. Physically beautiful men—the glory of the race when it was young—are almost an anachronism now; and we may wonder whether, at some time or other, physically beautiful women may not be an anachronism likewise. (Book Third, Chapter 1)

It is quite clear that Hardy as narrator is intruding into the story here. He tells us that in future man must see 'life as a thing to be put up with' and that this point of view will be reflected in the wrinkles on his face.

He tells us that physical beauty is now out of date. While his comment may serve as an apology for Clym's appearance, which it is not meant to, it in no way develops the plot. Instead there is a lull in the action while Hardy reflects and preaches. Hardy does not usually intrude in such an awkward way. More often the reader is conscious of him behind the scenes ordering and manipulating.

Some of the characters even talk the way we might expect Hardy to talk; some characters talk like actors in a third rate film. In Book Third, Chapter 4, there is a conversation between Clym and Eustacia:

> '. . . 'I loved another man once, and now I love you.'
> 'In God's mercy don't talk so, Eustacia!'
> 'But I do not think I shall be the one who wearies first. It will, I fear, end in this way: your mother will find out that you meet me, and she will influence you against me!'
> 'That can never be. She knows of these meetings already.'
> 'And she speaks against me?'
> 'I will not say.'
> 'There, go away! Obey her. I shall ruin you. It is foolish of you to meet me like this. Kiss me, and go away for ever. For ever—do you hear?—for ever!'

This dialogue is dreadful. It sounds like something out of cheap magazines. It is bad because it is so overdone and melodramatic with the characters striking such self-conscious poses. Eustacia sees herself as some kind of tragic heroine making the grand gesture. Her words do not suit the occasion and the effect is ludicrous. The reader scoffs and moves on. In Book Third, Chapter 3, Clym and Eustacia have been discussing the puncture she suffered in church. This is part of their first conversation:

> . . . 'Would you like to help me—by high-class teaching? We might benefit them much.'
> 'I don't feel quite anxious to. I have not much love of my fellow-creatures. Sometimes I quite hate them.'
> 'Still I think that if you were to hear my scheme you might take an interest in it. There is no use in hating people—if you hate anything, you should hate what produced them.'
> 'Do you mean Nature? I hate her already. But I shall be glad to hear your scheme at any time.'

A young man and a young woman, attracted to one another, simply do not talk in this grandiose way. The dialogue does not ring true. The effect is again melodramatic like Eustacia's gesture in Book First, Chapter 6, after she and Wildeve have been discussing their relationship: 'She seized the moment, and throwing back the shawl so that the firelight shone full upon her face and throat, said with a smile, "Have you seen anything better than that in your travels?"' The conversations of the rustics are consistently effective because they sound genuine and are full of local colour and idiom. There are flaws in the dialogue elsewhere.

The reader often feels that he is an observer looking on at what happens in the novel. He is not so much involved as he is an onlooker. It is part of Hardy's method to put him at a distance from the scene of the action. For example in Book First, Chapter 1, he sets the scene at a distance before his narrative eye moves closer to the old man on the road in Chapter 2. The same distancing effect is achieved in Chapter 3. 'Had a looker-on been posted in the immediate vicinity of the barrow, he would have learned that these persons were boys and men of the neighbouring hamlets.' Often he makes us see or hear things through the eyes or ears of characters in the novel. There is a great deal of eavesdropping in *The Return of the Native.* For example, the reddleman overhears the conversation of Wildeve and Eustacia at the pond, Eustacia overhears the furze-cutters talking about Clym, the boy overhears Wildeve and Eustacia, Eustacia overhears Thomasin, Mrs Yeobright, and Clym. Indeed the reddleman, Thomasin's guardian angel or not, acts as a spy throughout the novel. He is a sinister figure about whose inner workings we do not know much. Often, then, along with Hardy, we observe the development of human drama from a distance; often, with Hardy, we watch somebody else watching what is happening.

Hardy helps his slow plot to move by pointing forwards at the end of a chapter. This technique is necessary if a novelist is writing in serial form because it creates tension and makes the reader want to read on. One example will do. Diggory Venn, who means well in his blundering way, wins Mrs Yeobright's money back from Wildeve, and hands it all over to Thomasin not knowing that half of it was for Clym. Near the end of Book Third the novelist tells us '. . . it was an error which afterwards helped to cause more misfortune than treble the loss in money value could have done'. We wonder why and read on to discover that it leads to the fight between Eustacia and Mrs Yeobright, estrangement between Clym and Eustacia and Mrs Yeobright's walk across the heath. We wonder what would have happened if the reddleman had not interfered.

Hardy has a keen eye for detail and for completeness of character portrayal. The student may examine many sections of the novel to prove this point. In *The Return of the Native* there are many highlights, many great moments: the visual images of the heath and the sky, and the heath and the white road at the beginning; the dramatic appearance of Eustacia on Rainbarrow; the powerful Queen of Night chapter; the meeting of Clym and Eustacia under the eclipse of the moon; Clym's sense of oneness with his surroundings as a furze-cutter; Mrs Yeobright's walk to Clym's cottage and her haunting return journey; the games of dice on Egdon with the strangely evocative effects of glowworms, heath-croppers, and a candle and moth; the final argument between Eustacia and Clym before their separation; the timeless power of the heath itself; and the chaos of the wild night when Eustacia and Wildeve drown. Each of these bears close study. There are many other examples the student could choose.

Hardy planned *The Return of the Native* as a tragedy in five acts, the action of which takes place on Egdon Heath over a period of a year and a day. Each book deals with an action which appears to be complete in itself, like an act in a play. The novel first appeared as a serial. By the end of Book Fifth Mrs Yeobright, Eustacia, and Wildeve are dead, Thomasin is a widow, and Clym is left lamenting. '. . . my great regret is that for what I have done no man or law can punish me'. Then surprisingly there is a sixth Book called 'Aftercourses'. Hardy added this to please the readers of the magazine in which his novel was published. He provided them with a traditional happy ending. Thomasin and Venn are married. In 1912 Hardy said that

> the original conception of the story did not design a marriage between Thomasin and Venn. He was to have retained his isolated and weird character to the last, and to have disappeared mysteriously from the heath, nobody knowing whither—Thomasin remaining a widow.

It is left to the reader to choose the ending he prefers: 'Readers can therefore choose between the endings, and those with an austere artistic code can assume the more consistent conclusion to be the true one.'

The novel has been tragic in tone throughout. Hardy is suggesting that those readers who adhere strictly to the rules of tragedy will prefer the conclusion that suits those rules. Since Greek tragedy was at the back of his mind in writing *The Return of the Native* Hardy's suggestion is that the reader of taste may prefer to ignore the last section. But of course tragedy does not necessarily end in gloom so that it is possible to justify a preference for the second conclusion. The choice and the argument are left to the reader.

The characters

In a letter to Arthur Hopkins, the illustrator, Hardy said: 'The order of importance of the characters is as follows—1. Clym Yeobright, 2. Eustacia, 3. Thomasin and the reddleman, 4. Wildeve, 5. Mrs Yeobright.'

Clym Yeobright

The rustics mention Clym Yeobright first in Book First, Chapter 3. We learn that he is 'wonderful clever' and that he is coming home because of Thomasin's marriage. Mrs Yeobright had forbidden the marriage in the church because she did not approve of Wildeve. Fairway suggests that Clym should marry Thomasin himself. Captain Vye later tells Eustacia that he remembers Clym as 'a promising boy', and in conversation with Humphrey and Sam (Book Second, Chapter 1) he offers the opinion that Clym should never have left Egdon to become a diamond merchant in Paris because he disapproves of family changes. What was good enough for the father is good enough for the son. We also learn that Clym is a thinker and for that reason has 'strange notions'. Our first impressions of Clym are being formed by other characters before he actually appears.

We see him through the eyes of Eustacia at the Yeobright party. It is his face which commands attention because 'it was really one of those faces which convey less the idea of so many years as its age than of so much experience as its store'. Eustacia is doing the observing; Hardy is doing the thinking. His face shows that 'thought is a disease of the flesh'. Eustacia finds his presence disturbing.

Hardy presents Clym Yeobright as the young man of the future, as modern man, in Book Third, Chapter 1. He is not physically beautiful. His face expresses 'the view of life as a thing to be put up with'. His experience is recorded in his face. People had always expected something of him, something out of the ordinary because he was not one 'to stand still in the circumstances amid which he was born'. The rustics do stand still. They never change. They eat, work, play, and sleep. In that sense Clym is somebody special—perhaps even an outsider. There are others in the novel. Eustacia has come from Budmouth to Egdon; Wildeve has come from engineer to innkeeper; Diggory Venn from farm to reddleman; Clym from Paris to his native soil.

As the Sunday morning haircut is in progress in front of Fairway's house the locals wonder why Clym has not returned to Paris yet. Clym turns up and explains that he had always thought of Egdon as a place not worth bothering about because life on it was contemptible. But when he lived in Paris he realised that he was trying to be like people who had nothing in common with himself. He was trying to live a new life which was no better than life on Egdon. For him it became worse. He felt depressed because he thought his business was the most effeminate work in the world. Clym explains to Fairway and the others that he wants to study to get qualifications as a teacher and then to open a night-school on or near Egdon.

Again the voice of truth and authority comes from the rustics when Clym leaves:

> 'He'll never carry it out in the world', said Fairway . . .
> 'Tis good-hearted of the young man,' said another.
> 'But, for my part, I think he had better mind his business.'

We know what to expect. So do the locals. They have struck an ominous note. Something unpleasant will happen. We know and they know.

Hardy leaves nothing to the imagination in his analysis of Clym's character in Book Third, Chapter 2. Clym has an idea. He thinks that his fellow men want knowledge which will give them wisdom rather than money. He thinks that the people on Egdon will be keen to be taught for that reason. Blind to reality, he is intent on pursuing his goal. The simple fact is that the local people would not consider any type of education unless it offered worldly advance. Besides, they are set in their own ways of living. Clym's idea reflected the thinking of men in cities such as Paris. He is unlucky. 'The rural world was not ripe for him.' He is ahead of his time. Country people are not yet ready for such notions. They much prefer luxury to culture. His idea, then, is false. Clym is deceiving himself. He has created an illusion which will shape his destiny. His ideal cannot exist. Eustacia is deluded too, of course, in the picture of Paris she creates in her imagination and in the image of Clym she creates for herself. Clym's mind is not well-proportioned. He has the zeal of a fanatic in abandoning his business and in hoping to help the natives on Egdon. He behaves like an evangelist.

It is strange that someone who knows the heath so well, that someone who is its product, should not understand its inhabitants. Clym loves the heath. It is part of him:

> His eyes had first opened thereon; with its appearance all the first images of his memory were mingled; his estimate of life had been coloured by it; his toys had been the flint knives and arrow-heads which he found there, wondering why stones should 'grow' to such odd shapes; his flowers, the purple bells and yellow furze; his animal kingdom, the snakes and croppers; his society, its human haunters. (Book Third, Chapter 2)

He belongs to Egdon physically, instinctively, emotionally; he is remote from Egdon intellectually because, in Hardy's novels, thinking is so often a disease that warps, disables and kills. Mrs Yeobright warns him that his fancies will ruin him, that he is pursuing a backward course. Why should a successful businessman want to be an impoverished schoolmaster? She wants him to do well. She cannot make him see and he cannot make her see. His belief is that men are born to misery and he wants to teach them how to endure it. The irony of the situation is that Clym is creating his own misery by believing this because studying at night causes his temporary blindness and separation from Eustacia. What happens to him is not something imposed by the gods or Fate. Without realising it, he creates his own tragic situation. Hardy does, however, make the point that Clym was born at the wrong time—too soon for his ideas to be successful.

In their first lengthy conversation in Chapter 3 Clym asks Eustacia if she will teach too. The idea has no appeal for her. Hardy tells us that he 'had reached the stage in a young man's life when the grimness of the general human situation first becomes clear; and the realisation of this causes ambition to halt awhile'. Clym believes Eustacia is an educated woman who could help him in a school; Mrs Yeobright, however, believes Eustacia is lazy and dissatisfied. The reader can see that Clym is naive and foolish.

During the eclipse of the moon the lovers break their passionate embrace to talk about their feelings for one another:

> 'Has it seemed long since you last saw me?' she asked.
>
> 'It has seemed sad.'
>
> 'And not long? That's because you occupy yourself, and so blind yourself to my absence. To me, who can do nothing, it has been like living under stagnant water.' (Book Third, Chapter 4)

There is dramatic irony in these words of Eustacia. Clym likes to be busy and later will blind himself with his work; Eustacia cannot settle to do anything, as Mrs Yeobright knows, and later will meet death by drowning. Hardy has a habit of pointing forward to future events. This helps to keep the plot moving. Clym loves Eustacia with all his heart. She fears that passion such as theirs will not last: 'Nothing can ensure the continuance of love. It will evaporate like a spirit.' She is right. The dialogue again points forward to future events.

The tone of the words is gloomy, melancholic. Clym proposes to her, and instead of giving him a direct answer, she keeps talking about Paris. A few months later Paris is to come between them and help to destroy their marriage. Eustacia promises to marry him and hopes that he will give up his ideas of education so that they can go to Paris. The dialogue is rather solemn for a pair of lovers in the full bloom of passion. Eustacia, however, does know herself: 'Sometimes I think there is not that in Eustacia Vye which will make a good homespun wife.' Again she is right. When is Clym ever right? They agree to live in a tiny cottage for six months before moving to Budmouth. Clym guarantees that it will not be longer than that 'if no misfortune happens'. 'If no misfortune happens,' she repeated slowly.

Instead of seeing Eustacia as a goddess Clym now sees her as a woman to support and fight for. He thinks he is being hasty 'but the card was laid, and he determined to abide by the game'. The gambling metaphor is appropriate in the context and we are probably reminded of it during the game of dice on the heath. 'Whether Eustacia was to add one other to the list of those who love too hotly to love long and well, the forthcoming event was certainly a ready way of proving.'

For a month they live in absolute solitude in a world of their own. Within another month their world is shattered. Eustacia has quarreled bitterly with Mrs Yeobright, Clym has gone blind, and Eustacia loathes her station in life. Her passion for Clym has gone but there remains some tenderness between them:

> 'I suppose when you first saw me and heard about me I was wrapped in a sort of golden halo to your eyes—a man who knew glorious things, and had mixed in brilliant scenes—in short, an adorable, delightful, distracting hero?'
>
> 'Yes', she said, sobbing.
>
> 'And now I am a poor fellow in brown leather.'

For once Clym is right. Eustacia's illusions have now vanished.

Clym feels responsible for his mother's death. He is prostrated by remorse. His despair kept reminding Eustacia of 'the spectre of a worn-out woman knocking at a door which she would not open'. Guilt and fear oppress her. Clym, unable to comprehend her inhumanity and treachery, confronts her: 'You shut the door—you looked out of the window upon her—you had a man in the house with you—you sent her away to die.' They tear at one another's nerve strings. The upshot is that from now on Clym means nothing to Eustacia. He feels responsible for Eustacia's death too, hating himself because no law can punish him. His mother's judgement was accurate: 'He should have heeded her for Eustacia's sake even more than for his own.' (Book Fourth, Chapter 3). The native who returned to Egdon is to spend the rest of his days preaching in a variety of places on 'morally unimpeachable subjects'.

Eustacia Vye

The most colourful character in the novel first appears as a mysterious figure of night, a natural addition to the summit of the Barrow. She disappears into the night as the furze-cutters shamble on to the scene to build a fire. Susan Nunsuch says that Captain Vye's grand-daughter is 'very strange in her ways'. Our first impression then, is that she is a lonely figure who does not belong to this environment. When the locals leave she returns.

She is tall, ladylike in her movements. She stands heedless and fearless of night. She utters a lengthy sigh that blends with the noises of the wind. She is holding something back. Hardy describes her profile as she raises the telescope to look at a window of the inn. '. . . it was as though side shadows from the features of Sappho and Mrs Siddons had converged upwards from the tomb to form an image like neither but suggesting both.' Sappho was a Greek poetess who drowned herself because of frustrated love; Mrs Siddons was a famous tragic actress. Hardy is quick to add that this is a superficial impression of her face but that impression lingers on.

Her manner is preoccupied, dreamlike, despondent. Her youthfulness is emphasised in her jumping up the bank of the pool. She laughs when Wildeve appears because she knows she has power over him. Their conversation shows quite clearly that she is in command of the situation. She requires his affection because it suits her capricious nature. Eustacia teases him and he teases her. She wants to be elusive, hard to get. The fire summoned him for her amusement. There is the suggestion that there is something witchlike in her power. The pair of them play a lovers' game.

Hardy draws a complete portrait of Eustacia in Book First, Chapter 7, Queen of Night. Eustacia belongs with gods and goddesses:

> She was in person full-limbed and somewhat heavy; without ruddiness, as without pallor; and soft to the touch as a cloud. To see her hair was to fancy that a whole winter did not contain darkness enough to form its shadow: it closed over her forehead like a nightfall extinguishing the western glow.

There is something exotic and romantic about her. She has style and beauty. At times she looks like the Sphinx, at times like a goddess. She has pagan eyes suggesting dark secrets; her perfectly formed lips suggest a deep passionate nature; her physical presence brings to mind the smell of rare roses, the richness of rubies, and the depth and colours of tropical midnights; her moods range from drowsy contentment to fiery restlessness; her movements are like the ebb and flow of the sea; in general she looks like Diana, Greek goddess of the moon, or the goddess of war, or the queen of the heavens. Egdon is hell for this goddess because there is no place on it for her 'celestial imperiousness, love, wrath, and fervour'. Although she hates the heath, the darkness of Egdon has become part of her. She is full of suppressed energy, hate, and love. She has the pride of appearance of a goddess condemned to spend her life in the Greek underworld.

Born in Budmouth, condemned to Egdon, and seeing few people, Eustacia allows her imagination to take over as she conjures up romantic pictures of summer days, military bands, officers, and bright colours. She has dignity and solemnity and suppressed vitality. She looks like a queen who has lost her kingdom yet in her loneliness she has the company of her inner world. On the outside she gives the appearance of being 'listless, void, and quiet' whereas on the inside she is busy thinking, feeling, imagining.

What she wants most of all is passionate love. She needs it as a cure for her isolation. 'On Egdon, coldest and meanest kisses were at famine prices; and where was a mouth matching hers to be found?' Egdon is physically and emotionally barren. Eustacia longs for passion and fulfilment. 'To be loved to madness—such was her great desire. Love was to her the one cordial which could drive away the eating loneliness of her days.' For her love must be a blaze, a fire. It matters not how long the fire lasts provided the heat of the moment is strong. She will remain faithful to a lover as long as that heat is strong. Eustacia knows that such a passion does not last long, she knows that unhappiness is always waiting for her, but she still wants and needs love to quench her parched spirit.

To do what one is supposed to do goes against her nature. She is rebellious, gloomy, and original. Bored and irritable on Egdon, she feels that nothing is worth while. She pretends that Wildeve is somebody special only because there is nobody else around and she wants to relieve her boredom. Hardy says that her passionate nature combines the qualities of Heloise and Cleòpatra. It is noble and grand, and it is also selfish and destructive. She herself thinks that any love she may enjoy will run away quickly like the sand in her glass.

Eustacia has a youthful dream which she hopes to find fulfilled in Clym. Sam the turf-cutter said that 'her thoughts were far away from here, with lords and ladies she'll never know, and mansions she'll never see again'. She longs for what she calls life in Book Fourth, Chapter 6. She wants 'music, poetry, passion, war, and all the beating and pulsing that is going on in the great arteries of the world'. In other words she is creating a life through her imagination—a life that is divorced from reality because reality is Egdon. She yearns for such a life and yet is perpetually stalked by death. The very first present that Clym offers her is water; her last encounter on Egdon will be with water.

When Clym treats her as a murderer after his mother's death, she loses all feeling for him. Clym is cruel, inhuman. He does not want to hear her side of the story. She was only partly to blame. She should have answered the first knock. In Book Fifth, Chapter 3 Eustacia tells Clym that she has been wronged by him, that she has lost everything through him:

> 'All persons of refinement have been scared away from me since I sank into the mire of marriage. Is this your cherishing—to put me into a hut like this, and keep me like the wife of a hind? [a poor ignorant countryman]. You deceived me—not by words, but by appearances which are less seen through than words.'

There is some truth in this because Clym has always been able to do just what he wanted to do regardless of anybody else. He is self-righteous and single-minded. He assumes that what he decides to do must be the right thing to do. The other part of the truth is that Eustacia had formed a false impression of what he was like. Clym was at his happiest working and singing as a furze-cutter. It was then that her illusions were shattered. She often feels that fate or destiny is against her. At the end of Chapter 5 she is feeling so hopeless because 'To have lost is less disturbing than to wonder if we may possibly have won: and Eustacia could now, like other people at such a stage take a standing-point outside herself, observe herself as a disinterested spectator, and think what a sport for Heaven this Eustacia was.' We knew at the start of the novel that she had no chance of winning.

Her last appearance is on Rainbarrow where the darkness and the rain match her mood. 'Never was harmony more perfect than that between the chaos of her mind and the chaos of the world without.' As she bends down under the umbrella she feels as though a hand is drawing her into the Barrow. She wonders if she is to remain a captive on Egdon. There is no suggestion that she is thinking of killing herself. If anything, the suggestion is that Egdon will claim her. 'The wings of her soul were broken by the cruel obstructiveness of all about her.' She feels beaten down by the forces around her. There is no point in running away with Wildeve because he is not a great man and because she does not want to break her marriage vow. She cries in anguish and talks to herself as the rain pours down. There is no point in running away alone because she has no money and because time does not change. Every year she would be in the same wretched state. Eustacia feels that she has tried to be a 'splendid woman' but fate has been against her. She cries out in a frenzy of bitter revolt:

> 'I do not deserve my lot! O, the cruelty of putting me into this ill-conceived world! I was capable of much; but I have been injured and blighted and crushed by things beyond my control! O, how hard it is of Heaven to devise such tortures for me, who have done no harm to Heaven at all!' (Book Fifth, Chapter 7)

That is her point of view. What is Hardy's and what is yours? Do you think she is a tragic figure or just a flighty young girl? She goes on through the rain to her death in Shadwater Weir as her waxen image melts in the fire of Susan Nunsuch. Clym suspects that she has killed herself. Suicide or accident? Which form of death do you think suits the character of Eustacia and fits in with the theme, plot, and mood of *The Return of the Native* as a whole?

Thomasin Yeobright

To describe the kind of person Thomasin is, the student should consider the following: (*i*) the comments of the rustics in Book First, Chapter 3; (*ii*) the description of her in the reddleman's van in Chapter 4; (*iii*) what she says and does in Chapter 5; (*iv*) how she behaves under stress in Book Fifth, Chapter 8.

Damon Wildeve

His first name Damon suggests Demon. The locals refer to him in Book First, Chapter 3 as being almost as clever as Clym. He gave up his career as engineer to keep a public-house. In appearance he is a lady-killer. He is a gadabout, a butterfly: 'Altogether he was one in whom no man would have seen anything to admire, and in whom no woman would have seen anything to dislike.' After an affair with Eustacia he falls in love with Thomasin whom he proposes to marry. The fact that he makes a mistake over the marriage licence probably indicates that he is not very sure that such a marriage is right for him. Before that, he goes back to Eustacia when summoned. Then he decides to marry Thomasin to spite Eustacia who exchanges looks with him at the ceremony. When he learns that Eustacia is to be married he wants her again. There is a perverse or romantic streak in him: 'To be yearning for the difficult, to be weary of that offered; to care for the remote, to dislike the near; it was Wildeve's nature always.' (Book Third, Chapter 6). It is not that Wildeve is an evil man. He is proud and forthright, he runs a good business, he makes a reasonable husband. There are times when, sick of domestic life, he yearns for the passionate life he once had with Eustacia. He has an imagination just as active as Eustacia's. He offers to go with her, to flee from Egdon to far off places. He is suggesting a wild, passionate, adventurous life which he imagines is still possible. He was prepared to abandon Thomasin and family to achieve it, so he is morally and socially culpable.

The student should find the following passages useful in further developing his ideas of Wildeve: (*i*) The meeting of Wildeve and Eustacia by the pond in Book First, Chapter 6; (*ii*) Wildeve disagrees with Mrs Yeobright in Book First, Chapter 5; (*iii*) Wildeve and Eustacia walk on the heath they both hate in Book First, Chapter 9; (*iv*) The games of dice on the heath in Book Third, Chapters 7 and 8; (*v*) He dances with Eustacia in Book Fourth, Chapter 3; (*vi*) His visit to Eustacia as Clym sleeps on the floor in Book Fourth, Chapter 6; (*vii*) His behaviour over the inheritance in Book Fourth, Chapter 8; (*viii*) The last meeting of Wildeve and Eustacia by the pond in Book Fifth, Chapter 5; (*ix*) His last appearance in Book Fifth, Chapter 9.

Mrs Yeobright

Clym's mother is a lady of breeding. She is proud and 'thinks so much of her family respectability' that she is deeply hurt when Thomasin returns home unwed. She is haughty in manner and has a superior air. Hardy tells us in Book Third, Chapter 3 that 'she had a singular insight into life, considering that she had never mixed with it'. She gives the impression of being an aristocratic lady who is out of place on Egdon. Mrs Yeobright certainly never mixes with the locals. She is always at a distance. Her insight is instinctive. Clym is making a mistake by giving up his career in Paris and by marrying Eustacia Vye—she happens to know these things intuitively.

Between Clym and his mother there is a close bond of love. To outsiders it might appear that they are cold to one another. But theirs is the kind of absolute love that does not reveal its presence by word, gesture, or touch. When there is a disagreement or argument neither can make the first move to restore friendship. She warns Clym that Eustacia is lazy and dissatisfied. '"You are blinded, Clym," she said warmly. "It was a bad day for you when you first set eyes on her."' She is more accurate than she knew. Clym's studies will blind him for a while and his changed physical state will cause their later separation. What she says is usually the truth although she is unkind in calling Eustacia a 'hussy'. In her eyes she is no lady because ladies do not wander about heaths at night nor do they have affairs with people like Wildeve. She is not respectable, nor does she come of a respectable family. Mrs Yeobright shudders at the thought of her son marrying a Corfu bandmaster's daughter. In Book Fourth, Chapter 1, Eustacia says: 'It was a condescension in me to be Clym's wife.' That really sets Mrs Yeobright off. The sparks fly. She is merciless in her condemnation of Eustacia, whom she describes as idle and voluptuous. In her eyes Clym is wrong-headed and foolish because he ignores the advice of his parent. He seems determined to do the wrong thing. Mrs Yeobright may be right but she is also self-righteous because she tells the reddleman that she has forgiven Thomasin her marriage and has now decided to forgive Clym his marriage.

Mrs Yeobright has a strong will, she has tenacity of purpose, she has courage, and, opposed to her pride, she has humility. She makes the grand gesture in The Closed Door. Under almost impossible physical conditions she makes her way across the heath to her son's cottage, and believing that Clym has refused to let her in, she heads back for home. Mrs Yeobright dies of a broken heart and a snake bite.

Mrs Yeobright does not dominate the action of the novel. Indeed she does not make many appearances. She is a lonely person. We feel her presence when there is tension between Eustacia and Clym. We are conscious of her as a commonsensical figure.

The student should reread Hardy's description of Mrs Yeobright's meeting with the rustics in Book First, Chapter 3.

Part 4

Hints for study

The setting

The Return of the Native is set in Hardy's Wessex on Egdon Heath. The heath has existed for many centuries and has witnessed many calamities. It remains unmoved. Nothing or nobody can disturb Egdon which is majestic and 'grand in its simplicity'. However haggard Egdon may be, it has a subtle appeal to a new breed of man who finds himself in harmony with sombre things. Clym Yeobright is at peace on Egdon. He belongs there. In winter the untameable heath has a solemn intensity with its storms and darkness.

> It was at present a place perfectly accordant with man's nature—neither ghastly, hateful, nor ugly: neither commonplace, unmeaning, nor tame; but, like man, slighted and enduring; and withal singularly colossal and mysterious in its swarthy monotony. As with some persons who have long lived apart, solitude seemed to look out of its countenance. It had a lonely face, suggesting tragical possibilities. (Book First, Chapter 1)

On the highest and loneliest part of Egdon is the barrow where Eustacia stands fixed as a necessary part of the heath. 'I cannot endure the heath except in its purple season. The heath is a cruel taskmaster to me.' Eustacia does not fear the heath. She hates it. Clym says 'To my mind it is most exhilarating, and strengthening, and soothing. I would rather live on these hills than anywhere else in the world.' Born and bred there, he is a part of Egdon: 'Take all the varying hates felt by Eustacia Vye towards the heath, and translate them into loves, and you have the heart of Clym.'

Their attitudes to Egdon create and point forward to the conflict between Clym and Eustacia which is at the heart of the novel. She yearns for the boulevards of Paris, for far-off romantic places; for her, Egdon is a prison and later a destructive force. He wants to educate the rustics, to do good deeds; for him, Egdon is home and later redemption. For Egdon, which has the function of a leading character in the novel, their human problems do not exist. Egdon has 'a face on which Time makes but little impression'. Time has made an impression on Clym's face. '. . . it was really one of those faces which convey less the idea of so many years as its age than of so much experience as its store'. Hardy presents Clym as a thinker and his face expresses it. He may have much in common with Egdon but he does not have permanence.

We are always conscious of the presence of Egdon. It dwarfs the people who live on it. It is not a symbol. It is there and it is oppressive. See Book Third, Chapter 5, where as Clym watched Eustacia walking away

> the dead flat of the scenery overpowered him . . . There was something in its oppressive horizontality which too much reminded him of the arena of life; it gave him a sense of bare equality with, and no superiority to, a single living thing under the sun.

Egdon Heath is dominant, lasting—a forbidding presence. When Clym finds out through Johnny Nunsuch that his mother had visited him before her death he feels insignificant rather than angry. In Book Fifth, Chapters 2 and 3, instead of thinking of Eustacia and her male visitor he was conscious that 'there was only the imperturbable countenance of the heath, which, having defied the cataclysmal onsets of centuries, reduced to insignificance by its seamed and antique features the wildest turmoil of a single man'. That is the general tone of the novel as the major characters seem to battle against insuperable odds on Egdon's heathery world. An air of fatality is always present on the heath which has many moods. It can be savage, beautiful, and impassive.

For the self-effacing, warm, compassionate Thomasin there is nothing grim, supernatural or evil about Egdon Heath. Like Clym she is at home on it. She makes her way through the storm with her baby at the climax of the book:

> To her there were not, as to Eustacia, demons in the air, and malice in every bush and bough. The drops which lashed her face were not scorpions, but prosy rain; Egdon in the mass was no monster whatever, but impersonal open ground. Her fears of the place were rational, her dislikes of its worst moods reasonable. (Book Fifth, Chapter 8)

She is matter-of-fact and clear-headed. Her feet are on the ground. The nature of the characters in the novel is frequently demonstrated by the heath.

Egdon's age and history diminish the importance of characters, too, because they appear like specks on a vast and difficult landscape that has always been there. Near the end of the novel Clym walks alone on the heath imagining the people who used to live there. They had all lived and died there. The tone is wistful, nostalgic. Clym and the others are but one moment of Time in the history of Egdon. As the novel closes Clym stands in Eustacia's position on the barrow to preach to the people —a haunting reminder, full of sadness.

When we think of Egdon we think of dancing, furze-cutting, The Quiet Woman, local beliefs and superstitions, bonfires, history, time, and the reddleman who seems to be everywhere. We may also think of some of the most memorable scenes in the novel—the meeting of Eustacia and Clym under the eclipse of the moon, the gambling scene, Mrs Yeobright's walk across the heath on a hot day, the drownings at Shadwater Weir.

For those reasons Egdon Heath is a major force in *The Return of the Native*. Hardy frequently describes in detail particular features of the heath. For example, in Book Third, Chapter 5, Clym has had a bitter argument with his mother about Eustacia. He feels hurt because he loves his mother and cannot accept her disapproval of Eustacia. In Chapter 6 he goes in search of a cottage where he and Eustacia can set up house. On the way he comes upon a plantation of fir and beech trees:

> The wet young beeches were undergoing amputations, bruises, cripplings, and harsh lacerations, from which the wasting sap would bleed for many a day to come, and which would leave scars visible till the day of their burning. Each stem was wrenched at the root, where it moved like a bone in its socket, and at every onset of the gale convulsive sounds came from the branches, as if pain were felt.

The pain Hardy attributes to the trees reflects the pain of Clym. Their suffering seems to make Clym's suffering greater. Because they heighten and focus attention on Clym's anguish they make Clym's personal feelings dramatic. The description as a whole is ominous because it points forward to further suffering. While Clym and the trees suffer, Egdon is in its element: 'Those gusts which tore the trees merely waved the furze and heather in a light caress. Egdon was made for such times as these.'

The book is full of such examples. It is a story-telling method that comes naturally to Hardy. In Book Fourth, Chapter 5, Mrs Yeobright reaches a hill near Clym's house after a long walk across the heath. She feels exhausted and ill as she sits down under the fir trees. She is anxious and tense because she desperately wants to be friends with Clym and Eustacia again:

> Not a bough in the nine trees which composed the group but was splintered, lopped, and distorted by the fierce weather that there held them at its mercy whenever it prevailed. Some were blasted and split as if by lightning, black stains as from fire marking their sides, while the ground at their feet was strewn with dead fir-needles and heaps of cones blown down in the gales of past years.

This description suggests suffering and death. It highlights Mrs Yeobright's predicament and creates a strong feeling of sadness or pathos. She is lonely. She feels rejected by her own son. The description as a whole adds to the air of misery and foreboding in this part of the novel. In Chapter 6 on her way home she sits down feeling completely isolated and prostrated. She thinks her son has rejected her. She thinks that the sun is waiting to destroy her. Then Hardy describes a colony of ants and the flight of a heron. The effect is to make her an even more pathetic and lonely figure. This and other examples are worth close examination.

Examination questions on *The Return of the Native* should be designed to test your knowledge and understanding of the novel. In any novel worth reading there are passages which are guides to the theme; there are passages which describe or develop character; there are passages that are turning-points; there are passages that are dramatic highlights; there are incidents or episodes that express conflict; there are deliberate contrasts between scenes or characters; there is dialogue to throw light on character and develop plot and theme; and there is setting that reflects the tone and mirrors the theme of the novel as a whole.

What do you think merits close study in *The Return of the Native*? What are you going to remember most about the book in a few years' time and why? What are the novel's qualities, highlights or characteristics? Which passages or incidents should you study closely?

(1) The description of Egdon in Book First, Chapter 1 and elsewhere.

(*a*) 'Every night its Titanic form seemed to await something; but it had waited thus, unmoved, during so many centuries, through the crises of so many things, that it could be only imagined to await one last crisis—the final overthrow.'

The passage suggests the power and the timelessness of the heath, it creates an atmosphere of apprehension or suspense, and it establishes a solemn tone.

(*b*) 'Haggard Egdon appealed to a subtler and scarcer instinct, to a more recently learnt emotion, than that which responds to the sort of beauty called charming and fair . . . for the storm was its lover, and the wind its friend.'

The heath has a wild beauty. It is untamed and permanent with a dour independence. It has the cragginess of Clym's face in Book Third, Chapter 1.

(*c*) 'It had a lonely face, suggesting tragical possibilities.'

It reminds us of Eustacia, and Hardy says it is like man because it is 'slighted and enduring'. The main characters in the novel suffer. Life is something to be endured.

(2) The introduction of Eustacia Vye, Book First, Chapters 6 and 7.

(*a*) 'Eustacia Vye was the raw material of a divinity.'

(*b*) 'She was in person full-limbed and somewhat heavy; without ruddiness, as without pallor; and soft to the touch as a cloud. To see her hair was to fancy that a whole winter did not contain darkness enough to form its shadow; it closed over her forehead like nightfall extinguishing the western glow.'

She is probably Hardy's most exotic or romantic creation. Queen of Night is one of the striking chapters in the novel.

(*c*) 'Her presence brought memories of such things as Bourbon roses, rubies, and tropical midnights; her moods recalled lotus-eaters and the march in Athalie; her motions, the ebb and flow of the sea; her voice, the viola.'

Can such a person be real? Does Hardy overdo the portrait?

(*d*) 'Seeing nothing of human life now, she imagined all the more of what she had seen.'

She has a vigorous imagination which she uses to combat Egdon. She conjures up a picture of Budmouth on a sunny day and out of Clym she creates a knight with whom she falls in love.

(*e*) 'To be loved to madness—such was her great desire. Love was to her the one cordial which could drive away the eating loneliness of her days. And she seemed to long for the abstraction called passionate love more than for any particular lover.'

That is a key passage in the novel because it highlights what Eustacia is and it makes clear her dilemma which will have an inevitably tragic outcome.

(3) The introduction of Clym Yeobright, Book Second, Chapter 6; Book Third, Chapter 1.

(*a*) 'He already showed that thought is a disease of the flesh, and indirectly bore evidence that ideal physical beauty is incompatible with emotional development and a full recognition of the coil of things.'

This is a central theme in the novel. The face of Clym, who is modern man in an ancient setting, is lined with the marks of thought and knowledge of life (. . . 'a full recognition of the coil of things . . .'). Ideal physical beauty is not possible if man thinks. That is what Hardy means by 'thought is a disease of the flesh'.

(*b*) 'As for his look, it was a natural cheerfulness striving against depression from without, and not quite succeeding.'

The 'depression from without' again refers to his awareness of things. Were he not aware or conscious of life and living he would be by nature cheerful. Consciousness and thought are diseases. There is marked contrast between Clym and the rustics who live naturally.

(*c*) 'The view of life as a thing to be put up with, replacing that zest for existence which was so intense in early civilisations, must ultimately enter so thoroughly into the constitution of the advanced races that its facial expression will become accepted as a new artistic departure.'

Hardy enforces the points made already.

(*d*) 'The only absolute certainty about him was that he would not stand still in the circumstances amid which he was born.'

When the native returns to his birthplace he is educated and wants to change things. He is an idealist out of touch with people and their needs. Had he never left Egdon, had he been able to stay where he was, there would have been no tragedy. He would simply have carried on living like the others. As a boy Clym was a restless spirit of promise.

(*e*) 'Clym had been so inwoven with the heath in his boyhood that hardly anybody could look upon it without thinking of him.'

Other characters identify him with the heath. In Paris he found that life was no better than life on the heath and that decided him.

(*f*) 'I would give it up and try to follow some rational occupation among the people I knew best, and to whom I could be of most use.'

As one of the Egdon men said: 'I think he had better mind his business.' Examine Book Third, Chapter 2 in detail.

---

(4) The relationship between Eustacia and Clym.

(*a*) They meet after the play (Book Second, Chapter 6).

(*b*) The student should examine their conversation after the well incident (Book Third, Chapter 3).

(*c*) They embrace under an elipse of the moon (Book Third, Chapter 4).

'Nothing can ensure the continuance of love. It will evaporate like a spirit, and so I feel full of fears.'—Eustacia.

The student should consider the conversation about Paris and marriage. Clym perceives that '. . . she loved him rather as a visitant from a gay world to which she rightly belonged than as a man with a purpose opposed to that recent past of his which so interested her.'

'How terrible it would be if a time should come when I could not love you, my Clym!'

(*d*) They arrange the wedding (Book Third, Chapter 5).

(*e*) Trouble brews in their domestic bliss (Book Fourth, Chapter 1).

(*f*) They exchange bitter words. Examine closely Book Fourth, Chapter 2 and see the end of Chapter 4.

(*g*) The student should note the tension of Clym's remorse and Eustacia's guilt (Book Fifth, Chapter 1).

(*h*) They separate (Book Fifth, Chapter 3). This is the climax of the novel. What happens after happens because of this dramatic scene.

---

(5) The reddleman: The student may find it useful to employ the following material to discuss his function in the novel.

(*a*) Hardy introduces this strange character in Book First, Chapter 2. We first see Eustacia through his eyes. He has rescued Thomasin from an awkward situation. We wonder why. He learns from Johnny Nunsuch that Eustacia met Wildeve by the pond. Venn is very interested and we wonder why.

(*b*) Book First, Chapter 9 gives the history and describes the occupation of the reddleman. Hardy says that if you were to look at this reddleman you might guess 'that good-nature, and an acuteness as extreme as it could be without verging on craft, formed the framework of his character'. He loves Thomasin and overhears the meeting of Eustacia and Wildeve. In Chapter 10 he tries to persuade Eustacia to give up Wildeve. In Book Second, Chapter 7, he delivers gifts and a letter from her to him. After the wedding he disappears from the heath for some months.

(*c*) He reappears in Book Third, Chapter 7 and Chapter 8. When he wins all the money from Wildeve he unknowingly moves the plot in a new direction. He did not know that half of it was for Clym. Mrs Yeobright thinks that Wildeve has passed it on to Eustacia without Clym's knowledge. Eustacia, who knows nothing of the inheritance, thinks she is being accused of accepting presents from a former lover. Look at what happens later as a result of Venn's mistake.

(*d*) He tries to keep Wildeve away from Eustacia in Book Fourth, Chapter 4. Here he is like the traditional reddleman whom children fear.

(*e*) In Book Fifth, Chapter 2 he gives Clym vital information about his mother's forgiveness and intended visit.

(*f*) He has a wash and marries Thomasin.

---

(6) The rustics of Egdon: what is their function in *The Return of the Native*?

(*a*) The student should re-examine the bonfire sequence (Book First, Chapter 3).

(*b*) Humphrey and Sam build a stack of furze-faggots (Book Second, Chapter 1).

(*c*) The student may find it useful to reread the description of the hair-cutting outside Fairway's house (Book Third, Chapter 1).

(*d*) The student should consider Sam's comment on Eustacia (Book Third, Chapter 2): 'I should rather say her thoughts were far away from here, with lords and ladies she'll never know, and mansions she'll never see again.'

(*e*) The student may find it useful to examine the characters Susan and Johnny Nunsuch, Christian and Grandfather Cantle, and Charley.

(*f*) Mrs Yeobright's death scene (Book Fourth, Chapter 7) should not be ignored.

After a study of these suggestions the student could make the following points, each of which should be developed and illustrated:

(*i*) The rustics are part of Egdon, they accept Egdon, and belong there.
(*ii*) They eat, work, play, and live without thinking about it. What is meant to be is meant to be. It is not their business to try and change anything.
(*iii*) They have a natural vitality. A dance and a jug are good fun.
(*iv*) They talk common sense and they are also superstitious.
(*v*) They reflect the history, customs, legends, beliefs, and folklore of an ancient Wessex.
(*vi*) They lead simple, uncomplicated lives.
(*vii*) Hardy uses them to introduce main characters.
(*viii*) They are the voice of truth.
(*ix*) In the voice there is often an ominous note, a warning.
(*x*) They serve as messengers and servants.
(*xi*) They comment on the action of the novel.
(*xii*) They are in marked contrast to the principal characters who cannot be content and who torment one another.

Hardy does not idealise them. He presents them as they are. The dialogue is refreshing, convincing, and, at times, difficult.

Examination questions

General advice

(1) Read the question carefully.
(2) Answer the question directly. Do not have a prepared answer.
(3) If there are two or three parts to the question spend as much time on each in your answer unless you can show that one part is more important than the others. Sometimes a question will indicate how much time to spend on each part.
(4) From the novel select material that you can use to answer the question.
(5) List the main points you wish to make in the plan for the answer and support each one with reference to or quotation from the material you have selected.
(6) Make the conclusion a direct answer to the question.
(7) Read your answer very carefully. Check everything. Remember that a quotation must make sense on its own.

Specimen questions

(1) Account for the separation of Clym and Eustacia. ('Account for' means 'give reasons for'.)

Main points:
(*i*) Clym discovers that Eustacia did not open the door to his mother.
(*ii*) In his fury he says things that cannot be unsaid.
(*iii*) She retaliates by abusing him.
(*iv*) Eustacia's nature—Paris, romantic longings, knight and her imagination.
(*v*) The seeds of trouble in their early relationship—his idealism.
(*vi*) Marriage arrangement—love in a hut.
(*vii*) She is disillusioned with Clym as peasant and social failure.
(*viii*) The whole tone of the book suggests that the two main figures will not have happy futures.

Arrange in an order that is logical and chronological. Build up to the climax: (*viii*), (*iv*), (*v*), (*vi*), (*vii*), (*i*), (*ii*), (*iii*). Point (*viii*) goes first as a general introduction to establish the atmosphere.

We know that *The Return of the Native* will end in tragedy from the very beginning. The narrative pace is slow; the language is solemn, formal, and ponderous; the ominous presence of Egdon Heath seems to dominate everything; there are frequent hints of impending disaster. It is in the characters themselves, as well as in the setting, that we find such hints.

The first reason for the separation of Clym and Eustacia is to be found in the very nature of Eustacia. Her imagination works hard. 'To be loved to madness—such was her great desire . . . she seemed to long for the abstraction called passionate love more than for any particular lover.' She is in love with the idea of passionate love and depends on her imagination to create it. When she hears of Clym's return to the heath her imagination makes him into a fascinating knight. She then falls in love with the product of her imagination rather than with the real Clym who knows that she loves him 'as a visitant from a gay world.' Eustacia has romantic longings for Paris. Clym knows and is foolish to continue seeing her. Mrs Yeobright is right. They cannot help themselves. One day Eustacia's illusions will vanish and so will her love for Clym.

Clym's idealism is another reason. His feet are not on the ground. He has grandiose ideas of improving the lot of the peasants. She wants to go to Paris; he wants to educate the people. They agree to marry on the understanding that in six months they will move to Budmouth. The seeds of estrangement are there from the beginning. He is going in one direction, she in another.

When Clym loses his sight and becomes a furze-cutter Eustacia's dreams are shattered. Her husband, the knight in shining armour, is now a peasant in a brown outfit who is happy to be a peasant. She regards him as a social failure. After an exchange of bitter words she says: 'I have still some tenderness left for you.' Her passion is spent. A further cause of disharmony is the bitterness between Eustacia and Mrs Yeobright.

Because Eustacia did not open the door for his mother, Clym regards her as being responsible for her death. 'You shut the door—you looked out of the window upon her—you had a man in the house with you—you sent her away to die.' He is furious at her treachery, abuses her in a vile way, searches her desk for letters, and accuses her of infidelity. She accuses him of exaggeration and blames him for the wretched life she now lives: 'You are nothing to me in future . . . You deceived me—not by words, but by appearances . . .' Of course it was Eustacia who deceived herself by imagining that Clym was an exciting being from another world. Clym chastises himself for being bewitched by her, and we naturally think of Susan Nunsuch making her wax effigy. Eustacia confesses that she 'wilfully did not undo the door the first time she knocked.' In her eyes that is the extent of her crime. She refuses to identify Wildeve. Clym wants nothing to do with her until she does: 'And when you will confess to me the man I may pity you.' They part in bitterness. The next time he sees her she is dead.

For these reasons Clym and Eustacia separate; for these reasons *The Return of the Native* has a tragic outcome.

(2) Describe briefly any dramatic scene in the novel. Then discuss its importance in the novel as a whole.

That means: what light does it throw on character, plot, and theme.

Suppose you choose Mrs Yeobright's walk to the unopened door. Because the question says 'briefly' you should spend no more than two or three paragraphs describing her walk across the heath to the door and the situation inside the house. What is the importance of this scene in the novel as a whole?

(*i*) It is sad and ironic that Mrs Yeobright who came to make the peace should be sent away.
(*ii*) It is a grand gesture on her part.
(*iii*) She is a pathetic broken-hearted figure.
(*iv*) There is a contrast between the shabby Clym and the neat Wildeve.
(*v*) The scene dramatises the relationships of Clym, Eustacia, Wildeve and Mrs Yeobright.
(*vi*) Clym's stirring in his sleep is a good example of Hardy's love of coincidence or melodrama.
(*vii*) The scene marks a turning-point in the plot. Why? What effect does the discovery have on Clym and on Eustacia? What happens then?
(*viii*) Several tensions or conflicts have brought this scene about. What are they?

(3) 'How I have tried and tried to be a splendid woman, and how destiny has been against me!' cries Eustacia on the heath. Does she bring about her own fate or not? Argue a case.

In general you might argue that what happens in the novel happens because the characters are the kind of people that they are. Character determines action. To argue a case, then, you will need to describe and discuss Eustacia and show that she determines what happens to her. Tired of Wildeve, she seeks out and marries Clym; tired of Clym she chooses flight. But she cannot escape from herself. Does anything happen to her just by chance?

(4) Why did Hardy call the novel *The Return of the Native*?

This question invites you: (*a*) to show that everything in the novel turns on Clym's return to Egdon, and (*b*) that Clym is the central figure in the novel.

Hardy's main interest is Clym Yeobright. A character sketch or analysis will be the main part of the answer. To answer (*a*) you will need to discuss the relationships of the main characters and refer to major events.

(5) Compare and contrast the following pairs of characters: Damon Wildeve and Clym Yeobright; Thomasin and Eustacia.

Such a question invites you to give a character sketch of each and to emphasise differences.

(6) Describe in detail an episode that you thoroughly enjoyed in *The Return of the Native.* Why did you enjoy it?

This more personal question is a variation of question 2. It asks you to spend most of the essay describing an episode. Why did you enjoy it? Now you are expected to say something about the quality of the writing. You might consider narrative style, characterisation, development of plot and theme, atmosphere, tension, conflict, special effects.

(7) Describe a scene in which the interaction of the characters develops a theme or idea in the novel.

Suggested choices:

(*i*) Clym's argument with his mother shows that he is foolish to fall in love with the lazy and voluptuous Eustacia and that he has lost touch with reality. There is no place for his ideas and ideals on Egdon. He has created an illusion.

(*ii*) As Damon and Eustacia talk, Clym lies asleep on the floor in his furze-cutter's clothes. Eustacia, feeling sorry for herself, sees a different Clym to the one she created in her imagination. She has created an illusion which is now shattered.

(*iii*) The mutual abuse and recriminations of Book Fifth, Chapter 3 show the two main characters confronted with reality. Dreams have been shattered. Clym now sees Eustacia through his mother's eyes.

A reminder: What the examiner wants most of all is your response to what you have read. Say what you think.

Part 5

Suggestions for further reading

The text

HARDY, THOMAS: *The Return of the Native*, ed. Derwent May (The New Wessex Edition), Macmillan, London, 1974. There is a paperback of this edition.

Biography

GITTINGS, ROBERT: *Young Thomas Hardy*, Heinemann, London, 1975. *The Older Hardy*, Heinemann, London, 1978

OREL, HAROLD: *The Final Years of Thomas Hardy 1912–1928*, University Press of Kansas, Lawrence, 1976.

Background

WILLIAMS, MERRYN: *Thomas Hardy and Rural England*, Macmillan, London, 1972.

Criticism

Each of the following books has a chapter on *The Return of the Native* which you may find useful.

GREGOR, IAN: *The Great Web*, Faber, London, 1974.

KRAMER, DALE: *The Forms of Tragedy*, Macmillan, London, 1975.

STEWART, J.I.M.: *Thomas Hardy: A Critical Biography*, Longman, London, 1971.

THURLEY, GEOFFREY: *The Psychology of Hardy's Novels*, University of Queensland Press, St. Lucia, Brisbane, 1975.

The author of these notes

Stewart Luke was educated in schools in Dundee and Arbroath. He read Honours in English at the University of Adelaide, South Australia. For ten years he taught English literature and languages in secondary schools and for ten years he lectured at Torrens College of Advanced Education, Adelaide, where he was Senior Lecturer in English, a position he now holds at the Adelaide College of the Arts and Education. He has published book reviews and various literary articles.